THE ART OF
FLORIDA

A Guide To The Sunshine State's Museums, Galleries, Arts Districts, And Colonies

RODNEY AND LORETTA CARLISLE

T0352459

Pineapple Press, Inc.
Palm Beach, Florida

Pineapple Press
An imprint of The Rowman & Littlefield Publishing Group, Inc.
4501 Forbes Blvd., Ste. 200
Lanham, MD 20706
www.rowman.com

Distributed by NATIONAL BOOK NETWORK

British Library Cataloguing in Publication Information Available

Library of Congress Cataloging-in-Publication Data
Names: Carlisle, Rodney, 1936- author. | Carlisle, Loretta, author.
Title: The art of Florida : a guide to the Sunshine State's museums, galleries, arts districts and colonies /
   Rodney and Loretta Carlisle ; photographs by Loretta Carlisle except where otherwise indicated.
Description: Palm Beach, Florida : Pineapple Press, 2021. | Includes bibliographical references. | Summary: "A
   visual guide to approximately 20 Florida art colonies and districts. The book will discusses in detail a variety
   of towns in Florida renowned as 'Art Colonies,' together with several 'Arts Districts' in both small towns and
   larger cities that have been designated by the local government and/or by developers as neighborhoods set
   aside to foster the arts. Many of the communities sponsor annual art festivals or shows that have been held
   for more than 40 years. The book features color photographs that capture the variety of art forms that are
   uniquely Florida and covers special aspects of art in Florida such as the great number of Florida artists, the
   influence of arts projects and social realism of the New Deal, mural painting in Florida, the 'Highwaymen,'
   and the extremely rich 19th and 20th century history of Florida artists. Colonies and districts include:
   Bradenton Village of the Arts, Eau Gallie Arts District, St Petersburg Warehouse Arts District and Central Arts
   District, Tampa and Tallahassee" —Provided by publisher.
Identifiers: LCCN 2021011016 (print) | LCCN 2021011017 (ebook) | ISBN
   9781683342588 (paperback) | ISBN 9781683342595 (epub)
Subjects: LCSH: Art museums—Florida—Guidebooks. | Art galleries,
   Commercial—Florida—Guidebooks. | Artist colonies—Florida—Guidebooks.
   | Art—Florida—Guidebooks. | Florida—Guidebooks
Classification: LCC N511.F6 C37 2021 (print) | LCC N511.F6 (ebook) | DDC
   708.1759—dc23
LC record available at https://lccn.loc.gov/2021011016
LC ebook record available at https://lccn.loc.gov/2021011017

♾️™ The paper used in this publication meets the minimum requirements of American National Standard for Information
Sciences—Permanence of Paper for Printed Library Materials, ANSI/NISO Z39.48-1992

Contents

Introduction

This book is organized around twenty-five art towns that survive to the present that have museums, galleries, studios, and art centers, and especially those with an active population of artists. Several of the towns are notable for special art destinations or events, such as a designated art district (Eau Gallie in Melbourne and Village of the Arts in Bradenton); historical art centers (New Smyrna Beach, Fernandina Beach, Bradenton, Maitland, and Key West); important art museums (Winter Park, Orlando, Naples, Ocala, Jacksonville, St. Petersburg, Fort Pierce, and Lakeland); important and widely attended annual shows (Mount Dora and Miami); or, in the case of Lake Placid, numerous murals documenting the town's history. The book is arranged geographically, by region and town.

This book is written as a guide to art in Florida, both art on display in museums and in public spaces such as sculptures and murals, and art for sale, in art galleries and at art shows. In addition, we describe a number of other art facilities, such as art centers where classes are offered to the public, residency programs for artists, and major annual art shows. In Florida, major art centers are found in most of the communities we discuss. Each of the art center programs is unique, with some giving more or less emphasis to gallery display, to classes for children or adults, to periodic juried or curated shows. Some offer residency programs to visiting artists.

In sidebars throughout the text, we present brief descriptions of the life and work of major, internationally known artists who made their homes in Florida, as well as major art programs at Florida colleges and universities that have national standing.

The term "art" is sometimes ambiguous; the word can refer to all of the arts including literature, drama, music, and other performing arts, as well as the pictorial arts. Here we use the term in a more narrow sense. We seek to describe where art in the form of the visual arts (such as painting, drawing, and sculpture) is created, is on display, or is on sale in the state of Florida.

Florida is a destination for artists, and the state has a rich history of welcoming outsiders, some of them outcasts or refugees from elsewhere, from the Seminoles who fled from Native American and white enemies in Georgia and Alabama, to African American slaves seeking freedom under Spanish rule or with the Seminoles, to generations of Americans who simply sought to escape the rigors of northern winters, either as perennial "snowbirds" or as permanent migrants. Among the many diverse settlers in Florida since it became part of the United States in 1821 were some who wanted milder winters and a less expensive place to live, and others who sought a place that accepted the unorthodox and the innovative, including many individualistic painters, sculptors, artisans, and writers. The internationally famous writers who lived in Florida in the nineteenth and twentieth centuries included Harriet Beecher Stowe, Marjorie Kinnan Rawlings, Ernest Hemingway, and John MacDonald. The list of famous painters and sculptors who chose to live in Florida is also extensive and includes those mentioned in this volume like Earl Cunningham, Doris Leeper, Albin Polasek, and Robert Rauschenberg, all of whom were inducted into the Florida Artists Hall of Fame. These are only some of the most notable of hundreds of successful artists, writers, and other creative workers who lived or resettled in Florida.

Many of the communities discussed in this volume have long-standing reputations as art colonies. The colonies were communities or neighborhoods where artists and writers congregated in order to establish settlements of like-minded, creative individuals. They were often notorious as places for men and women who sought to escape from towns and cities whose cultural atmosphere seemed to them to stifle creativity and enforce conformity of behavior. Like "colonists" among the "natives," artists in the nineteenth- and twentieth-century art colonies often sought to find remote villages or even urban neighborhoods, where unconventional lifestyles and creativity would be at best welcomed, or at least ignored. While such escape to special communities as colonies flourished in the late nineteenth century and through the first decades of the twentieth century, in recent years many of the so-called bohemian values shared by artists of that earlier period have become more widespread in Western culture, with a "live and let live," less judgmental attitude toward the lifestyle choices of others. Even so, in the present era, many practicing artists tend to congregate and settle in specific neighborhoods of larger cities, or in particular small towns, creating echoes of the era of art colonies. So, scattered through Florida, a state that has been built and settled by outsiders from its earliest times, visitors still find communities that thrive and take pride in a local art colony atmosphere. This is particularly true of some of the smaller communities covered here, such as Safety Harbor, Mount Dora, Eau Gallie, New Smyrna Beach, and Bradenton, as well as Key West.

In the case of towns and cities with a large art presence, we describe a bit of the local history of the town and then present in some detail the museums, galleries, and other features such as shows and art centers found in the present time, or the displays of murals, such as those found in Lake Placid, Safety Harbor, and St. Petersburg.

The towns are grouped in five regions:

Northwest: Pensacola, Tallahassee

Northeast: Fernandina Beach/Amelia Island, Jacksonville, St. Augustine, New Smyrna Beach, Eau Gallie and Melbourne, Fort Pierce

Central: Gainesville, Ocala, Winter Park, Maitland, Orlando, Mount Dora, Lakeland, Lake Placid

Gulf coast: Tampa, St. Petersburg, Safety Harbor, Bradenton, Sarasota, Naples

South Atlantic coast and Key West: Delray Beach, Miami, Key West

HOURS

We have not included the hours and regularly scheduled days that different museums and galleries are open because they are so subject to change. Many museums and galleries are not regularly open on Mondays, because they maintain open hours on Sundays for the convenience of visitors, but this practice is by no means universal. We provide phone numbers (as of 2020) so that visitors planning out-of-town trips to specific museums and galleries can verify scheduled dates, hours of operation, fees, and special events. A few museums close on occasion for wedding receptions, membership meetings, or other special closed or invitational gatherings, so verifying opening times in advance is always a good idea if a trip is planned. Furthermore, some museums have dates with special discounted rates of admission (which vary), and that can also be checked by phone. Through much of 2020, galleries and museums were closed because of the COVID-19 pandemic; we made our visits to most of the communities, museums, and galleries in the period December 2019–February 2020.

GALLERIES

While it might seem self-evident, there is an important distinction between a gallery and a museum. Galleries offer the art for sale, while museums retain the art and only offer some select reproductions and other items for sale in associated museum shops. Museums sometimes have special collections on temporary loan from private individuals or other museums, and almost all rotate some collections from storage to display and back every few months. One unique museum that opened in 2020, in Sarasota, plans to operate with no permanent collection of its own, but only with items on loan from other institutions.

Art galleries offer the art for sale, usually (not always) with the price, normally set by the artist, posted with the art on display. Museums display the art, usually with a small placard with the name of the artist, the years of his or her life span, and the name of the piece of art and its date of production; sometimes included is a comment on the significance of the piece of art in a larger context of the artist's life or in the history of the *genre* or type of art, or, occasionally, detailing the history of the particular item of art itself. Art centers are usually places where art classes are held, but many of them maintain a gallery-style presentation with works for sale, as well as spaces for classes. We have been careful to make such variations and distinctions explicit in our descriptions of the wide variety of facilities we researched and visited. A confusion sometimes arises because many museums refer to their display rooms as "galleries," but that does not imply that the art in those museum galleries is for sale.

In addition, many communities have an active group of practicing artists who participate in weekly, biweekly, or monthly studio tours, during which the public can observe them in their homes or studios, at work. Sometimes visitors on these tours are able to arrange to buy art directly from the individual artists. We have noted a number of these studio tours in various communities.

Seventeen of the communities maintain one or more active art centers. Art centers vary a good deal in the programs, but most offer classes to the public in arts and crafts; some provide studio space on a rental basis to artists. A unique Atlantic Center for the Arts in New Smyrna Beach has a whole campus and a large program for visiting artists in residence. Although no comprehensive history of American or Florida art centers has been written, local evidence in Florida suggests that some of the state's local art centers have long histories, dating back to the New Deal era or even earlier.

The art gallery scene changes from year to year. The forty-nine major art museums and more than two hundred galleries we discuss in detail were open and thriving in late 2019 and early 2020. Before planning a specific visit (especially a long trip), it would be wise to check current hours of specific galleries, centers, and museums by phone. Many galleries are owned and operated by a single artist-entrepreneur, so it is understandable that posted hours are only a guide to usual practice, not a commitment to a rigid schedule.

ART MUSEUMS

There are several different types of art museums among the fifty Florida museums discussed in this volume.

Some were established by a single individual or family who, after years or decades of art collecting, donated their personal collection to establish a museum, sometimes personally funding the design and construction of the museum structure itself.

A second type of museum is owned and operated by a governmental entity, such as a municipality, county, or state agency.

A third type of affiliation is academic. Some of these are operated by a college or university for teaching purposes; some include galleries for display of faculty and student work but are also open to the public. Further, a number of small and large personally or community-funded museums have become affiliated with local colleges or universities.

A fourth type is a museum that is operated by a local or community non-profit entity; some of these are devoted either exclusively or primarily to the works of a single artist.

In some cases, a museum originally based on a personal collection has reorganized to be operated by a government agency or by a new local nonprofit entity, and in these cases the new management usually makes an effort to document and respect the taste and nature of the original private collector and to build the collection with the founder's goals in mind. All of these museum types are nonprofit entities, although almost all operate small museum shops as profit centers. In addition to the fifty major museums detailed in the main text, we provide a listing of eighteen smaller Florida art museums, with contact information, at the end of the text, pages 199–200.

A number of the towns we describe in this book have "gallery districts," areas of a few blocks in which several art galleries are found clustered nearby. Most gallery owners believe this practice is very useful, as potential customers visiting one gallery are likely to visit neighboring galleries. Such neighborhoods are found in Key West, Bradenton, Naples, Melbourne/Eau Gallie, Sarasota, Mount Dora, and Miami. This clustering of one type of business in specific neighborhoods is, of course, common in many cities around the world, where garment districts, jewelry districts, or antique-shop districts, among others, are convenient both for customers and for retailers who benefit from walk-in shoppers. For art shoppers and visitors interested in art, the presence of such gallery districts is a distinct advantage, and we have identified them here with street directions.

ART COLONIES

The notion of artists as colonists moving to an established community, often a small rural town, and establishing a community within a community traces back to a group of French painters in the years 1830–1870, who moved from Paris to the nearby rural community of Barbizon. As individuals who sought to escape from the more formal artistic environment of Paris, and to paint outdoors, rather in studios, the colonists had a reputation as nonconformists. Their notion of painting outdoors, plein air, was made possible by the development of oil paint prepared in lead tubes (like toothpaste), and by portable easels for holding the work in progress.

The somewhat rebellious reputation of the Barbizon school appealed to the Romantic sensitivities of the era, and soon artists in other countries, including the United States, began to establish similar colonies. Among the early colonies in America were Provincetown, Massachusetts; New Hope, Pennsylvania; and Yaddo in upstate New York. These were joined later by Taos, New Mexico, and Carmel, California, among numerous others.

During the interwar years from 1919 to 1941, American art colonies attracted not only painters and sculptors, but also writers and others who sought an independent lifestyle; that "rebel" or "free lifestyle" reputation of art colonies has lingered a bit in the public mind. Few of the 1920s–1930s Florida "colonies" continue to the present—one of them is Key West. Another Florida town that had an art colony reputation in the interwar years was St. Augustine, but with the coming of World War II, that repute declined, and one author has designated St. Augustine as the "Lost Colony."

Several of the towns in this book have developed a strong art presence because of concerted planning efforts: Key West was originally consciously supported as an art colony by one of the New Deal programs of the federal government, enhanced by the presence of an internationally famous writer, Ernest Hemingway. New Smyrna Beach developed largely because of the effort of one patron and artist, Doris Leeper. In other cases, local governments have sponsored and encouraged a local art community, notably Melbourne/Eau Gallie, Bradenton, and, to an extent, Delray Beach. The reasons for the rise and development of artist-residential districts and art gallery shopping districts vary from place to place, often with unique causes.

Some of the communities in Florida with a reputation for attracting artists have changed in atmosphere because of their success. That is, after some towns developed a reputation for welcoming artists, real estate values later increased to the point that the town has become less affordable for beginning artists. This process of gentrification can be seen, for example, in Winter Park and nearby Maitland. There appears to be a cycle at work in such communities, similar to patterns seen in European art colonies and in some of the older colonies in the United States, such as Carmel, California, or Taos, New Mexico. In these towns, the stylish connotations of art and sometimes the success of individual artists has made the community a resettlement destination for wealthy art patrons and others. Their presence then raises real estate values, making it difficult for beginning artists to find or afford studio space and residences. And, of course, the increase in real estate values in Florida because of its attraction to migrants from the North goes on whether or not a town has had an early reputation as a haven for artists.

A NOTE ON MURAL ART

Outdoor mural art on the formerly blank walls of commercial buildings and warehouses comes in many forms in the present era. In some cases, the art is very much a reflection of local events and history. This is particularly the case in Lake Placid, where the dozens of murals offer depictions of local historical scenes and locally prominent individuals. More common elsewhere in Florida, however, is the use of murals to display the skill of the individual artist, in depicting panoramic scenes, abstractions, or iconic figures such as animals, sea life, or famous individuals. Some mural art reflects abstract, surrealist, or postmodern trends such as graffiti art, or echoes of the art styles of Latin America, Haiti, Africa, or Asia. Some murals are not signed, while others are signed with cryptic initials or icons. We have identified the mural artists whose works we photographed for this book. The largest collection of murals in the state is found in St. Petersburg, while Lake Placid has dozens of murals, mostly focused on local history and the local environment.

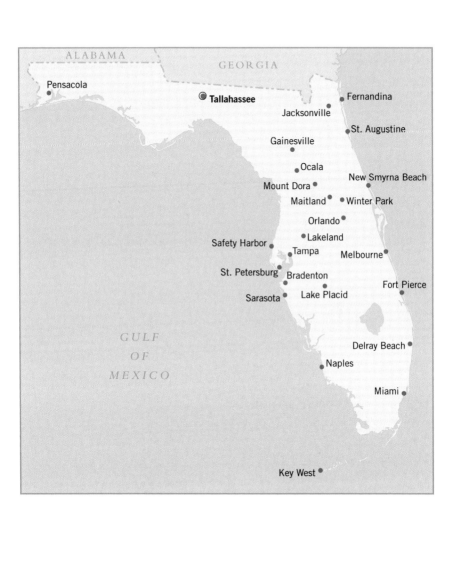

Pensacola Beach Water Tower. *Photo by Joe Ciciarelli on Unsplash*

PENSACOLA

MUSEUMS

Pensacola Museum of Art

The Pensacola Museum of Art is in a neighborhood with other cultural facilities and attractions including the Pensacola Children's Museum, the T. T. Wentworth Jr. Florida State Museum, and the Museum of Commerce, and is about two blocks to the west of Old Pensacola Village, a historic neighborhood that includes some twenty-eight or more restored historic buildings.

Pensacola went through a turbulent colonial history, like much of northern Florida, as the militarily significant locale and port played a part in the struggles between Spain and England for control of North America in the colonial period, between the United States and Spain for control of West Florida, and during the Civil War (1861–1865) as one of the major blockaded ports of the Confederacy. A visit to the nearby T. T. Wentworth Jr. Florida State Museum takes the visitor through the region's rich historical heritage.

The building that houses the Pensacola Museum of Art had its beginning as the city jail. Constructed in 1906–1908, the Mediterranean Revival style, twelve-thousand-square-foot building was the city's first permanent jail, serving from 1908 until 1954 when the city opened a new jail. Despite its impressive size, the building rarely held more than twenty-five prisoners at a time. Members of the local chapter of the American Association of University Women approached the

Among the unusual art events in Pensacola was this festival of colored umbrellas in the years 2017–2018. *Photo by Guy Stevens on Unsplash*

city with the possibility of leasing the city-owned building to house an art activities center and formed a new organization to promote the effort: the Pensacola Art Association. The city leased the building to the association for $1 a year, and for decades the former jail cells served as galleries for the display of art. In 1988, the association (reorganized as the Pensacola Museum of Art) purchased the building. In 2016, the association transferred the museum to the University of West Florida, and it is currently part of the University of West Florida Historic Trust.

The two-story museum presents changing exhibitions from year to year; exhibits sometimes focus on the work of one contemporary local Pensacola-area artist, on works of a single internationally known contemporary or historical artist, or on folk art or historical work of a particular culture. As examples of the wide-ranging selections in recent years, the museum has offered exhibits on contemporary paintings from the Peruvian Andes; selections from the prints of Aubrey Beardsley; and selections from the works of Gesche Würfel, who documented memories of Germany in World War II. In addition to such changing exhibits, every year the museum also hosts an exhibit of works by local members of the Museum Association.

Plan your visit: 407 South Jefferson Street, Pensacola, (850) 432-6247.

GALLERIES

The city of Pensacola hosts a number of art galleries that sell work by local artists (including three organized as cooperatives by artists), as well as a few galleries dedicated to fine art, that is, art that has gained a national or international reputation. The fact that the community art center and one of the cooperatives have operated for decades is testimony to the long-established nature of the local art community.

Artel Gallery

This gallery is a cooperative and serves as a community center as well as an outlet for members' art.

Plan your visit: 223 Palafox Place, Pensacola, (850) 432-3080.

Quayside Art Gallery

The works in this cooperative shop, established in 1973, are in a wide variety of genres; staff are member artists who volunteer their time at the shop.

Plan your visit: 17 East Zaragoza, Pensacola, (850) 438-2368.

Blue Morning Gallery

This gallery is also a cooperative with some sixty or more active members.

Plan your visit: 21 Palafox Place, Pensacola, (850) 429-9100.

Gumbo Gallery

This shop specializes in African American–themed items, and customers note the fairly frequent turnover of items on offer.

Plan your visit: 314 North DeVilliers Street, Pensacola, (850) 437-0025.

Marty Campbell Gallery

This shop offers work by local artists and also provides framing services.

Plan your visit: 3092 Gulf Breeze Parkway, Pensacola, (850) 565-4230.

Karin Gudmundson Fine Art
Also known as Gallery 1060, this gallery, located inside the First City Art Center in Suite E, specializes in the work of Karin Gudmundson and has also held juried exhibitions. Ms. Gudmundson was born in Hawaii, grew up in California, and had a career as a biologist before expressing herself as an artist in mixed media and acrylic paintings.

Plan your visit: 1060 Guillemard Street, Suite E, Pensacola, (850) 982-5142.

FIRST CITY ART CENTER

For more than seventy years, Pensacola has supported a community art center. Like other community art centers, the nonprofit First City Art Center, established

Surfboards as decorative art. *Photo by Nico Bhlr on Unsplash*

in 1949, offers classes and displays the work of local artists for sale, and leases studio and gallery space to artists as well. The center is decorated with several large murals, including one featuring butterflies, painted by Cindy Mathis, who has had mural commissions in New Orleans and Mississippi as well as in the Pensacola area.

Plan your visit: 1060 Guillemard Street, Pensacola, (850) 429-1222.

TALLAHASSEE

Tallahassee, the capital city of the state of Florida, was established in 1824 as the territorial capital, as a compromise between the two major settlements, St. Augustine and Pensacola, that had been established by the Spanish during the colonial era. Despite some efforts by leaders in other towns to move the capital, Tallahassee remained the capital of the territory (1824–1845) and then the state of Florida in 1845, to the present time. The city has a large population of temporary residents and people who moved to Tallahassee from elsewhere, as a combination capital city and college town, with two major universities and a large community college.

The city has an active art scene. In addition to working studios and galleries that host student work at Florida State University, there is a ten-acre art district

W. Stanley Proctor (1939–)

W. Stanley Proctor was born in Tallahassee in 1939 and has achieved national recognition as a sculptor. Self-taught, he started as a painter and has worked in clay, marble, and bronze. As a youth he enjoyed painting outdoors, and his paintings of animals, flowers, and landscapes were selected in juried shows. His works were shown in museums in the United States and Britain.

He attended Washington and Lee University in Virginia and, in 1960–1961, served as an aide for Florida member of Congress James A. Haley and Senator Spessard Holland. By the 1970s, Proctor began to concentrate on sculpture, with a focus on wildlife and human figures, increasingly focusing on work in bronze. By the 1980s and 1990s, he had received many commissions, and his works have been on display not only in Tallahassee, but across the United States. One of his works, Bandanna, *was presented by Lawton Childs, governor of Florida, to President Bill Clinton and remains on display in the White House. He has also done numerous works of sports figures.*

Although his works are found in many locations in Tallahassee, Proctor has had commissions around the United States. For example, he has completed two lighthearted interactive sculpture arrangements for the Mason County Sculpture Trail, based in Luddington, Michigan. In one of the works, a stump is provided for people to sit and join a sculpted group of father and son fishing as a photo opportunity; in another group, a line of sculpted children in a "follow the leader" procession leaves a spot for a living child to join in.

Proctor still lives in Tallahassee, where his children help manage the business side of his productive artistic career.

known as Railroad Square that has several working studios and two art galleries, along with a variety of other shops. In addition, the nonprofit LeMoyne Art Center conducts a range of art activities for children and adults. Scattered around the city rather than concentrated in a single arts district, there are about another ten art galleries, including cooperative, single-artist-owned, as well as proprietor-owned types. As in other Florida communities, new galleries open from time to time, but the presence of the Museum of Fine Arts at Florida State University, the LeMoyne Art Center, the number of independent galleries, the available studio space both at the university (for students) and at studios at Railroad Square all contribute to a local arts community that is widely dispersed throughout the downtown city area and surrounding shopping and residential areas.

MUSEUMS

Museum of Fine Arts, Florida State University

The Florida State University Museum of Fine Arts had its beginnings as the Fine Arts Gallery for Florida State University's School of Visual Arts. In 1971, the gallery moved into the new Fine Arts Building; it was renamed the Museum of Fine Arts in 1994. The university's Museum of Fine Arts has been accredited by the American Alliance of Museums and houses more than six thousand works by historical and contemporary artists. Some of the recent gifts have included works by internationally known artists such as

Robert Rauschenberg, David Levinthal, and Andy Warhol.

Plan your visit: 250 Fine Arts Building, 530 West Call Street, Tallahassee, (850) 644-6836.

Tallahassee Museum: Jim Gary Sculpture Exhibit

The African American sculptor Jim Gary (1939–2006), born in Florida, was a popular and internationally known artist of the late twentieth century. His unique medium was to weld metal junk, including automobile parts; used household utensils and tools; and small metal items such as nuts, bolts, and springs into fanciful shapes. Among his famous works is a collection he called *Creaturations* or *Twentieth Century Dinosaurs*, which represented full-scale dinosaur skeletons, welded together from junked auto parts and other scraps. He

Florida State University, Tallahassee

Florida State University offers BA and BFA degrees. The BA degree requires thirty credit hours in art and art history, while the BFA requires that two-thirds of the student's total course program (about 80 credit hours out of the total 120 credit hours for the degree) must be in art courses. The university also offers BA and MS degrees in art education, which qualify students to teach art in secondary schools, as well as PhD and EdD degrees that qualify graduates to teach art or art education at other universities. The program supports several museum-style galleries.

built them, he said, just because people liked them. Sometimes he would paint the sculptures; other times, he would leave the metal to naturally rust and weather. Gary preferred auto parts from older vehicles, because they had more character than new models, he said. He often would spend a whole day in a junkyard looking for the perfect piece.

Gary was born in Sebastian, Florida, and after his family moved to New Jersey, he went to work at age eleven to help support his family's meager resources. Attending public school and taking shop classes, he soon became adept at welding, building his own bicycle, and, later, building entire automobiles from junked parts. After service in the U.S. Navy, he taught welding in a vocational school and soon began exhibiting his

art. He gained national and international recognition in the 1960s after one of his sculptures of a life-sized woman was shown at a sidewalk show in New York, drawing widespread critical acclaim.

Gary's whimsical sculptures attracted large audiences and especially appealed to children. By the 1970s, *Jim Gary's Twentieth Century Dinosaurs*, a collection of some of his pieces, toured for extended stays at public parks and museums. Over the next decades, Gary's unique metal sculptures were shown widely in the United States and abroad, including a solo show in 1990 at the Smithsonian Museum in Washington, D.C.

Gary passed away in 2006. In 2009, a group of his supporters, led by his studio director, Kafi Benz, searched for a suitable spot for the permanent display

This dinosaur sculpture by Jim Gary is one of many at the outdoor Tallahassee Museum.

of the dinosaur collection and chose the Tallahassee Museum. The sculptures were moved there in 2011, where twenty-one of Gary's remarkable pieces are scattered throughout the outdoor museum exhibits.

Plan your visit: 3945 Museum Road, Tallahassee, (850) 575-8684.

GALLERIES

621 Gallery
This gallery is unusual in that it is a nonprofit operation. As noted in the gallery's mission statement: "621 Gallery is committed to bringing contemporary art, artists, ideas, and programs to the north Florida and south Georgia region. Monthly program offerings include monthly educational programming for children and adults, monthly literary readings, musical, theatrical and dance performances, as well as participation several times a year in outdoor festivals at Railroad Square Art Park." Among the financial supporters of 621 Gallery is the Boynton family, who originally established Railroad Square, as well as a number of local businesses. The gallery also plays a part in preservation and presentation of Railroad Square public art, such as a small sculpture garden.

Plan your visit: 621 Industrial Drive, Tallahassee, (850) 224-6163.

Southern Exposure Gallery/Feeling Art
This is a collaborative or cooperative gallery presenting the works of some seven members. The media include photography by Bill Humphries and other art media by B. Harper Frost, Thomas Thompson, Starr Shumaker, Katie Clark,

Lisa Cesare Jordan, and Francisco Verdacia. The membership changes with additions and retirements.

Plan your visit: 694 Industrial Drive, Tallahassee, (850) 933-3655.

Scattered around Tallahassee, there are another ten or so private galleries, with the number subject to change with additions and closures. Although these venues are not concentrated in a single arts district, the number and variety of galleries reflect Tallahassee's active arts community. The galleries are found in widely different neighborhoods, and they are listed here in alphabetical order, rather than by street or neighborhood.

American Folk Art Museum and Gallery
This gallery is located in the Tallahassee Mall. The gallery offers a collection of unique and prolific work of Mary Proctor. At the museum/gallery, some of pieces are not for sale. Ms. Proctor opened the gallery in the mall in 2011. She is a self-taught African American artist who has gained international fame for her works, some of which have been purchased and remain in the permanent collections of major art museums, including the American Visionary Art Museum, Baltimore, Maryland; High Museum of Art, Atlanta, Georgia; Mennello Museum of American Art, Orlando, Florida; Polk Museum of Art, Lakeland, Florida; Museum of Fine Arts, St. Petersburg, Florida; the Metropolitan Museum of Art, New York, New York; and the New Orleans Museum of Art, among others. Her works are not only unique in style but also in media, with pieces often made up of button-, fake jewel–, or

glass-encrusted figures upon a canvas of windows or doors, and sometimes include spiritual messages or comments.

Plan your visit: 2415 North Monroe Street, Tallahassee, (850) 443-4199.

Ash Gallery

Ash Gallery features art and jewelry and is situated in the heart of Frenchtown, the largely African American neighborhood that originally was part of the land granted in 1824 by the U.S. government to the Marquis de Lafayette, in recognition for his service in the American Revolution.

Plan your visit: 438 West Georgia Street, Tallahassee, (850) 510-5621.

Debortina

The name of this gallery is an anagram derived from the names of the two artist-partners, Debo Groover and Tina Torrance, and is located in the Indian Head neighborhood of Tallahassee, where all the streets have Seminole names. ("Chuli Nene" is "Pine Way" or "Pine Street" in English.) Ms. Groover earned an MFA degree in ceramics from the University of Georgia in Athens, Georgia, and she worked as a potter and itinerant teacher throughout the United States. Ms. Torrance earned an MS degree in rehabilitation counseling from Florida State University. The two met in the town of Monticello (just northeast of Tallahassee). In 2008, Ms. Groover developed a new art technique employing polymer clay in collage materials to produce framed artwork suitable for hanging. The response of collectors and buyers to this new and different art form was so positive that she and Ms. Torrance joined forces to form the Debortina Studio. Since that time, they have taken the artwork for display and sale to many art shows in Florida and in other states. In addition to their own studio-gallery in the Indian Head neighborhood of Tallahassee, they have also shown the work at Signature Art Gallery, which is noted separately below. The couple collaborates, with Debo making the works and traveling to the shows; Tina works both as manager of the gallery in Indian Head and also laying down the underlying, base layers in the ceramic paintings and building the frames.

Plan your visit: 1920 Chuli Nene, Tallahassee, (850) 321-3506.

M Gallery

Established in 1999, this small gallery offers already-framed prints and original art, as well as a line of gifts. The shop also offers framing services.

Plan your visit: 2533 Greer Road, Suite 3, Tallahassee, (850) 531-9925.

Signature Art Gallery

Mary Maida opened the Signature Art Gallery in 1996. Like several other local gallery owners and artists, she is a graduate of Florida State University, in this case with a degree in marketing. She entered the art field by arranging the sale of art to local businesses, including a bank, a law firm, and others. The staff at the gallery include graduates from various programs at FSU, including communications, art history, and education. The gallery is quite large, at four thousand square feet, and displays works from as many as fifty artists from all over the United States and Canada represented at any one time. Works include not only framed and unframed paintings and prints, but also a range of ceramics and small sculptures. The works offered for sale include "traditional, transitional, and contemporary works of art." The gallery has on staff both a master framer and a certified picture framer, and can provide a selection from a variety of frames with a wide price range. The shop provides, when desired, not only framing, but both painting and frame restoration. Clients have included private purchasers as well as law firms, hospitals, banks, and offices.

Plan your visit: 2782 Capital Circle NE, Tallahassee, (850) 297-2422.

1020 Art LLC

This unique gallery is the result of a collaboration between an artist and a building developer. The two-story office structure has glass atriums and winding stairs that display art and gifts. The collection is large, representing the work of more than sixty artists, with hundreds of items in a variety of media and styles. As well as paintings, the art includes jewelry, enamel, glasswork, carved boxes, and sculpture. The works on display include those of well-known contemporary American and international artists, with a focus on those resident in Florida. Prices are moderate to high. Somewhat unusual, the owners offer the building's conference rooms for business or organization meetings.

Plan your visit: 1020 East Lafayette Street, #202, Tallahassee, (850) 383-1020.

Venvi Art Gallery

This artist-owned gallery, opened in 2015, shows original work by about ten established artists, some of whom reside locally in Tallahassee. Originally from India, owner-artist Brinda Pamulapati studied under Jacob Pichhadze, a renowned Canadian artist, teacher, and gallery owner in Toronto, Canada. Ms. Pamulapati includes some of her own work in the Venvi Gallery; her works have also been shown at other galleries in Tallahassee as well as in Toronto. At the Venvi Gallery works are displayed against brightly lit white walls, enhancing the presentation of each item, very similar in style and quality of display to some art museum showings.

Plan your visit: 2901 East Park Avenue, Tallahassee, (850) 322-0965.

Vera Sorensen

This is the residence, studio, gallery, and classroom of Vera Sorensen. She was born in Ukraine and studied art in both Russia and Iceland. She has been offering classes in art since the year 2000.

Plan your visit: 825 Alliegood Avenue, Tallahassee, (850) 766-2662.

FLORIDA STATE UNIVERSITY GALLERIES

These galleries at Florida State University are more in the nature of museum displays of student work, rather than shops selling art. The university galleries serve both as studio/workspace for students and, on advertised occasions, as exhibition spaces for works to be shown publicly. Not incidentally, students gain experience in gallery management, maintenance, and publicity, as well as in the chosen art media itself. One of these galleries presents work of graduate students; the other provides space for undergraduates to display their work.

Working Method Contemporary Gallery

This dedicated gallery space is set up for MFA students at Florida State University, a program that in recent years has enrolled about thirty students. The space is for exhibition, experimentation, and documentation of their work while students. Some of the works are collaborative. From time to time, the gallery is opened on Fridays to host an exhibition open to the public—including not only paintings and sculpture but ceramics, video works, and performance art. The gallery is managed and operated by the students themselves.

Plan your visit: Carnaghi Arts Building, 2214 Belle Vue Way, Tallahassee.

Phyllis Straus Gallery

This is a space for bachelor of fine arts students to make and present "innovations, experimentation, and expression through exhibitions and events in contemporary art." Students submit work for selection for shows, which receive publicity and public attendance. A variety of events from artists, poets, musicians, and "like-minded creative individuals" are also scheduled. Students are responsible for the management and maintenance of the gallery space. The gallery was named after Phyllis Straus, who retired from her role as advisor to students in the Art Department at Florida State

University in 2007 and passed away in 2013. The gallery was at first situated in the Bachelor of Fine Arts Warehouse, a gallery in Railroad Square.

Plan your visit: Carnaghi Arts Building, 2214 Belle Vue Way, Tallahassee, (850) 339-3884.

ART CENTERS AND DISTRICTS

LeMoyne Art Center

The mission of the LeMoyne Art Center is "to promote and advance education, interest and participation in the contemporary visual arts." Operating since 1963, LeMoyne Art is a private, nonprofit organization supported by memberships and gifts. While operating as a gallery for a permanent collection that includes work by north Florida artists Karl Zerbe, Nancy Reid Gunn, and Fred Holschuh, among others, LeMoyne Art Center sponsors many other activities. These include lectures by visiting artists, arts and crafts classes for both adults and children, a free arts program for prekindergarten children, and rotating gallery exhibits with opening receptions. There is, in addition, a sculpture garden at the center.

Plan your visit: 125 North Gadsden Drive, Tallahassee, (850) 222-8800.

Railroad Square

Located just south of Tallahassee's Amtrak station, off Railroad Avenue, Railroad Square was formerly a ten-acre warehouse district owned by the McDonnel Lumber Company. The loop street of Railroad Square contained large warehouses, most dating back to the 1940s. In the 1970s, Nan Boynton developed the concept of converting the

At the entrance to Railroad Square, Tallahassee, visitors encounter this colorful shop.

warehouse district that her father had purchased as a real estate investment in the 1960s into an "arts community," by leasing the spaces to artists for studios, galleries, and other shops. She renamed the warehouse loop-street that made up the McDonnel Lumber Company property as "Railroad Square." The enterprise now rents space to about fifty shops, including, at present, two art galleries

and numerous artist studios. Other businesses in the years 2019–2020 ranged from a comic book store to a rock climbing gym and a brewery.

The working artists' studios in Railroad Square are opened to the public for tours on the "First Friday Gallery Hop." On the first Friday of every month, several food trucks and outdoor displays enhance the art-show atmosphere. The number of working studios varies from time to time, with several of them hosting the work of current or recent graduates of Florida State University's art program. This monthly set of tours offers a relatively rare opportunity for visitors to observe artists in their studios, see works in progress, and possibly purchase works directly from the artists.

Plan your visit: Industrial Drive, Tallahassee.

"Adaptive reuse" takes on a decorative flair in Railroad Square, Tallahassee.

FERNANDINA BEACH/ AMELIA ISLAND

Fernandina Beach is located on Amelia Island, at the northeastern tip of the state of Florida. Locally, residents take pride in calling Amelia Island the "Isle of Eight Flags," reflecting the turbulent early history of the area.

The island's location—at the border of Florida and Georgia—made it even less stable than other parts of north Florida that also went through several "flags," simply because as a frontier spot with an inland waterway port, it readily changed hands during Florida's long history. The eight flags over the island were the French, Spanish, and British flags during the colonial period. Then, in the early nineteenth century, the flag briefly fell under the control of other groups, each with its own flag. The Floridian/ Patriot forces represented an abortive effort of Georgians to liberate Florida from Spanish control in 1812. Gregor MacGregor, a British adventurer, briefly controlled the island in 1817 and flew a Green Cross flag. He was replaced by a Mexican pirate, Luis Aury, who was driven out by U.S. forces. During the American Civil War (1861–1865), Confederate forces controlled the island before it was returned to the jurisdiction of the United States during the Civil War. Here and there around Amelia Island, one can spot references to the eight flags, including an antique shop and a shopping center with the "eight flags" name.

Over the period 1980–2008, Amelia Island hosted an annual women's tennis match that drew thousands of visitors. From 1987 to 2008, the match had been sponsored by Bausch and Lomb (the Canadian-based contact lens company) and was held at the Cliff Drysdale Tennis Academy at Omni Resorts, Amelia Island, one of more than thirty Cliff Drysdale tennis resorts/academies in the United States and abroad. After 2008, the women's match was then held for two years at Ponte Vedra, but has not been held since.

In the twentieth and twenty-first centuries, Fernandina Beach has flourished as an active resort and retirement community. Fernandina Beach has developed a busy downtown with varied shopping, the "oldest bar" in Florida, excellent restaurants, and more than ten art galleries hosting the work of local, regional, and international artists. In the present period, the island's location—access to the sea, near the Georgia border, and quite accessible from Interstate 95—together with its balmy climate, has made the island a destination for tourists and attractive to artists, particularly those painting seascapes, beach scenes, and others working in the plein air tradition. The steady flow of retirees, tourists, and visitors has added to the active market for art.

There are several art galleries in town and nearby. Most notable, and the center of the community's art activities, is the Island Art Association Art Gallery and Art Education Center, which is open daily except for holidays. The association is a nonprofit cooperative, open to artists throughout Nassau County.

Although the Island Art Association has about two hundred members, due to the

limited space, only about fifty can exhibit their work at one time. The art is rehung every six or eight weeks, with some eighteen artists at a time competing for five spots to show their work in a juried process.

The day we visited, member artist John Abbott hosted the gallery, and he explained the working of the gallery and conducted a tour of the facility. John, a retired architect and now enjoying a second career as a painter, explained that the members of the association are drawn from all over Nassau County, not just from Amelia Island, but from other locales in the county to the west. Every member

Mosaic murals decorate the walls around the Amelia Island Association courtyard.

takes turns working in the gallery. The Art Education Center next door, to the rear of the courtyard, provides space for classes and workshops, so the association hosts not just a cooperative gallery, but a community art center as well.

The courtyard of the Island Art Association has an inlaid pattern of a chessboard, and we were fortunate to see the results of a recent project. John explained that thirty-two member artists contributed by each painting a separate chess piece to make up a full set, with the pieces about two feet in height, each piece a unique work of art.

The art center also arranges a high school February art show, with several participating schools in Nassau County

Member artists of the Amelia Island Art Association painted oversized chess pieces on display in the courtyard of the organization.

each submitting student work. John explained that the members of the association review art portfolios and award scholarships to promising students. The choice of winners is from a very large number of submissions, mostly painting, but also work in different media.

The art center participates in the "Artrageous Art Walk" offered 5:00 p.m. to 8:00 p.m. on the second Saturday of each month, April to September. In the fall and winter season months—October through March—the art walk is a bit earlier, 4:00 p.m. to 7:00 p.m. The tour includes not only the art center but eleven other galleries, studios, and shops listed below. The wide variety of galleries in downtown Fernandina Beach and

surrounding areas attests to the active art scene on the island.

Plan your visit: 18 North Second Street, Fernandina Beach, (904) 261-7020.

GALLERIES

Fern and Dina's

This shop not only hosts works by local artists but unique pieces by regional and international artists. Included in the items sold are ceramics, art glass, original paintings, and prints. The shop also includes a classroom where a variety of workshops and classes are held, as well as containing some studio space for rent to other artists.

Plan your visit: 26 South Fifth Street, Fernandina Beach, (904) 261-5566.

Art on Centre

This gallery offers a variety of works, including sculpture, glass art, and a variety of paintings by local, national, and internationally known artists, including many seascapes and shore pictures, at a "wide range of price points."

Plan your visit: 503 Centre Street, Fernandina Beach, (904) 624-7255.

Blue Door Artists

This is a cooperatively owned gallery, located on the second floor, approached by a gaily painted blue door and staircase. The shop features the work of local contemporary artists, who work in a variety of media. The works include not only paintings, but gifts, jewelry, baskets, gourds, and gift cards. Some of

One of several galleries in Fernandina Beach that have puns in their name.

ON CENTRE

the artists in the collective also offer art classes.

Plan your visit: 205½ Centre Street, Fernandina Beach, (904) 556-7783.

2nd Story Gallery and Studios

This shop is located upstairs, over a toy store. Visitors regularly comment that this small shop, somewhat hidden away in its upstairs location, is well worth a visit.

Plan your visit: 5 South Second Street, Fernandina Beach, (904) 277-6676.

Trish's Slightly off Centre

This shop consists of a gallery and studios spread over five rooms. Similar to Fern and Dina's and 2nd Story, the name reflects a bit of wry humor, as the shop is located "slightly" off Centre Street. In addition to paintings, the shop sells ceramics made by the owner, Trish Tipton.

Plan your visit: 218-C Ash Street, Fernandina Beach, (904) 335-1817.

Seaside Gallery

Artist Julie Delfs operates this gallery and offers classes in the studio/shop, located about four miles from the downtown center of Fernandina Beach, and about a block from the oceanfront.

Plan your visit: 2022 First Avenue, Fernandina Beach, (904) 491-2180.

Carol Winner Art

This gallery shows the works of the owner, an oil painter who focuses on local landscapes and shore scenes. She also works in jewelry and mixed media, and she crafts handbags too. Nearly all the art in the gallery has been made by her.

Plan your visit: 218-B Ash Street, Fernandina Beach, (904) 583-4676.

The Seaside Gallery is located a block from the beach on Amelia Island.

Casey Matthews Fine Art
This is the studio and gallery of Casey Matthews and, aside from the art walk, is only open by appointment. Matthews's work is internationally recognized and has been featured in many publications.

Plan your visit: 813 South Eighth Street, Fernandina Beach, (904) 556-1119.

Clay Times Art Center
This center has several pottery studios; rents studio space; and offers classes in glass painting, wheel throwing, and other crafts and art media.

Plan your visit: 112 South Third Street, Fernandina Beach, (904) 624-5824.

Ink Art Gallery and Creative Studio
This gallery offers abstract art as well as locally made craft items.

Plan your visit: 308½ Centre Street, Fernandina Beach, (904) 497-4859.

Story and Song Bookstore Bistro
This bookstore and bistro participates in the "Artrageous Art Walk" on the second Saturday of each month. It is open daily and "celebrates" all the arts.

Plan your visit: 1430 Park Avenue, Fernandina Beach, (904) 601-2118.

MUSEUMS

Museum of Contemporary Art

This museum, affiliated with the University of North Florida, has a permanent collection with many interesting contemporary works, and a changing selection of exhibits.

One of the changing exhibits is shown as *Project Atrium*, often with an implied or explicit commentary on contemporary events. For example, in late 2019, a display put together by Romanian-born, Qatari-raised Sudanese artist Khalid Albaih, titled *Camp/Wall/Flock*, focused on controversial aspects of U.S.

immigration policy. In early 2020, regional artist Kedgar Volta installed *The Fragility of Promise*, a light installation made up of more than one thousand light-emitting diode (LED) fixtures.

The museum primarily collects works produced from 1960 to the present. Selections from the permanent collection of almost one thousand works, representing more than five hundred artists, are displayed not only to show the works to the public, but also for study and scholarly research. Since 2016, the museum has organized the collection, not on a chronological basis, but around six themes: Art as Social Commentary, the Evolution of Mark-Making, Material as

Modern room at the Jacksonville Museum of Contemporary Art.

Meaning, New Media, Process and Object Relationship, and Representation.

Among the unusual displays are two on the second floor, representing "modern" furnishings of a living room area of a home, including pieces from the 1940s through the 1990s. The assembled collection includes three items from the estate of Jacqueline B. Holmes, including an undated layered glass vessel designed by Etsuko Nishi, a 1943 digital print on paper, and a 1992 burgundy and metallic vase. Other items include a settee designed by Florence Knoll (1917–2019), made from heavy gauge steel with chrome finish and a solid wood frame. The "room" also includes a 1966 side table designed by Warren Platner (1919–2006), who, as noted in the accompanying text, was "one of the iconic designers of the modern era." This innovative way of presenting "modern" furnishing design is quite unusual and is characteristic of the museum's effort to communicate complex and interesting developments in art and design effectively.

The museum hosts a student artist in residence from the University of North

University of North Florida, Jacksonville

The University of North Florida administers the Museum of Contemporary Art in downtown Jacksonville. The university offers BA programs leading to degrees in several art disciplines: painting and drawing, printmaking, photography, ceramics, sculpture, art history, and graphic design and digital media.

Florida art program and displays the artist's work on the fifth floor.

The museum conducts a wide variety of community outreach programs, including a family day with live music; a literary arts festival; a "MOCA Holiday Market" with performances by the Jacksonville Symphony Orchestra; a New Years' Eve party with a disc jockey, open bar, art performances, and catered food; and a Chinese New Year celebration. Other community events include yoga classes and free showings of movies, as well as drawing classes and workshops.

Plan your visit: 333 North Laura Street, Jacksonville, (904) 366-6911.

Cummer Museum of Art

The Cummer Museum provides free parking on Riverside Drive directly across from the front entrance to the museum and also offers free admission on select days of the week. Visitors can call ahead for information regarding free admission dates.

The museum has more than five thousand items in its permanent collection, arranged in a series of galleries by period. The museum derives from the fortune of an early lumber businessman, Wellington Cummer, who moved from Michigan to Jacksonville in 1896. His son, Arthur Cummer, and Arthur's wife, Ninah

Cummer, built a lavish home on the banks of the St. Johns River in Jacksonville in 1902. After her husband's death in 1943, Ninah Cummer began expanding on the family collection of art, amassing some sixty pieces by 1958, the year of her death. In her will, she established a foundation to expand on the art collection and to house it on the family property. The current building, designed in an art deco style, was completed and opened in 1961.

On its opening, the museum displayed works from Ninah Cummer's own collection of sixty items, supplemented by loans of art from other museums. Over the years since, the museum's collection has

Cummer Museum of Art.

grown to more than five thousand pieces, including the ancient Egyptian Stele of Iku and Mer-imat from 2100 BCE through works of the present era. In addition to a special collection of seven thousand Meissen porcelain pieces collected by Ralph Wark and his sister Constance over more than four decades beginning in 1922 and donated to the museum in 1965, other donated and purchased items have included works by Peter Paul Rubens, Winslow Homer, and Norman Rockwell, among many others. Other groups of more than two hundred donated items include works by American artist Joseph Jeffers Dodge and a collection of Japanese prints from the nineteenth and twentieth centuries. Another large donated collection is 140 works by James McBey (1883–1959), a Scots painter and etcher. McBey gained fame during World War I for his etchings of T. E. Lawrence and Emir Faisal of Arabia, and through the years from the 1920s into the 1950s, he produced hundreds of etchings. The Cummer holds one of the largest collections of McBey's works.

The permanent collection at the Cummer is so large that the curators are able to arrange highly informative and well-organized displays of period works from ancient times through the Old Masters, as well as twentieth- and twenty-first-century pieces. The accompanying well-researched descriptions of each piece of art thoroughly place each item in its historical and artistic context. Sculptures are displayed in the courtyards and grounds of the museum.

The pleasant "Cummer Gardens" that slope down to the St. Johns River were severely flooded during Hurricane Irma in 2017. Although the area was later cleaned and debris removed, damage by saltwater to the soil has slowed the recovery of the gardens to their former splendor. However, visitors still enjoy the scenic and relaxing areas facing the river.

Plan your visit: 829 Riverside Drive, Jacksonville, (904) 356-6857.

ST. AUGUSTINE

As the oldest city in the United States, St. Augustine has a rich history, with a fort dating to the 1670s, and many Spanish colonial buildings dating well before the transfer of Florida to the United States in 1822. The city is the premier historical tourist destination in the state. In the late nineteenth century and early twentieth century, the town gained a repute as an art colony, but it declined during World War II (1941–1945). However, two of the many buildings that reflected the Mediterranean Revival and Middle East Revival architectural movements of the early twentieth century remain major attractions in the present. Although the "colony" reputation for attracting artists from the North may have declined, the city has a very active community of both artists and art dealers. St. Augustine supports several art galleries, with items in the price range suitable to the casual buyer or tourist, to prices representative of fine art galleries of the first rank. An active local art association represents and displays work of many local painters and other artists.

MUSEUMS

Lightner Museum

This museum is housed in the former Alcazar Hotel, one of two grand late nineteenth-century hotels built by Henry Flagler in St. Augustine in the period 1887–1889. The other was nearby: the Ponce de Leon. Flagler also purchased the Cordova Hotel, built by a local rival, Franklin Smith. That one, renamed the Casa Monica Hotel, still serves as a hotel, part of the "Grand Bohemian" group of hotels that specialize in presenting fine art in luxurious settings; the Ponce de Leon is now the campus of Flagler College. Henry Flagler, who had earned his fortune as an associate of J. D. Rockefeller in the founding of Standard Oil, went on to extend his own

Lightner Museum, St. Augustine.

railroad-and-hotel "empire" down the Atlantic coast of Florida, eventually to Miami and on to Key West by 1913.

The Alcazar was once connected to the Casa Monica by an over-the-street, enclosed pedestrian bridge. An unusual feature of the Alcazar building is its former indoor swimming pool, entered from the Grenada Street side of the building, which now houses a restaurant on the floor of the now-empty pool. When built, the swimming pool was claimed to be the largest indoor swimming pool in the world. The Café Alcazar, at the former "deep end" of the pool, is open for lunch in its unique setting. Two stories of surrounding galleries of the museum look down on the open area of the pool floor,

Looking up from the Lightner Museum courtyard.

which is often rented out as a wedding venue. The exterior of the building is itself an interesting architectural artifact of the era, with its towers, courtyards, decorated window settings, and many other Mediterranean Revival features.

The Alcazar Hotel building was purchased in 1947 by Otto C. Lightner, the publisher of *Hobbies* magazine. Lightner had a huge personal collection of a variety of objects, ranging from matchboxes to chinaware. He envisioned the hotel building as a museum to house his collection and installed a set of glass cabinets to contain the items. In 1950, two years after he opened the museum, he passed away and the city-managed collection fell into disrepair. The city finally restored the structure and opened it to house both the Lightner collection and numerous city government offices in 1973–1974.

The Lightner Museum now houses an eclectic collection of nineteenth-century decorative art pieces, including not only paintings and sculpted pieces, but also glassware, hooked rugs, Tiffany glass, furniture, and typewriters. Other unique pieces and small collections favored by Otto Lightner include "coquillage"—decorative pieces consisting of assembled seashells, painted and glued together to make small fanciful sculptures. A huge collection of salt and pepper shakers is held by the museum, with usually only a small proportion on display. The building itself, with its large and airy gallery spaces, often sparsely occupied by the collections that are tastefully set off by the bright walls and open areas, is itself an "artifact" of the Gilded Age period of elegant and conspicuous consumption, with the Mediterranean Revival structure in keeping with the personal tastes of Henry Flagler and the diverse collection reflecting the eccentric interests of Otto Lightner.

Plan your visit: 75 King Street, St. Augustine, (904) 824-2874.

Villa Zorayda

A block from the Lightner Museum is the Villa Zorayda, a small but highly unusual museum, and the premier example of the Moorish Revival phase of architecture and art collecting in Florida. Built by Boston millionaire Franklin Smith in 1883, the building used the then-innovative technique of poured concrete and included such touches as crenellated walls, similar to those found on medieval fortresses, and towers that emulated minarets found on Islamic temples.

Franklin Smith named the building Villa Zorayda, after one of the three princesses in Washington Irving's 1821

Villa Zorayda, St. Augustine.

book *Tales of the Alhambra*. Smith, who had traveled in Spain, is credited as one of the leaders of the late nineteenth-century and early twentieth-century American fascination with the Islamic world, its culture, and its architecture. The museum building features hand-painted tiles and wood panels, stained glass, and an interior central courtyard that displays many artifacts collected by Franklin Smith and by Abraham Mussallem, a dealer in antiquities and oriental rugs who was originally from Syria. Mussallem purchased the building from Smith in 1913, and the Mussallem family has continued to preserve the building and make it available to the public. Among the many unique treasures in the collection is the Sacred Cat Rug, said to be twenty-four hundred years old, made from the fur of Egyptian sacred cats.

Plan your visit: 83 King Street, St. Augustine, (904) 829-9887.

Flagler College, St. Augustine

Located in the oldest city in the continental United States, Flagler College is situated right downtown, in the former Ponce de Leon Hotel built by Henry Flagler in 1888. Flagler College offers a BA with a fine arts major, which consists of forty-four credits in required art courses and another eighteen credits in elective courses. The college also offers a BFA degree program, to which students are admitted on a competitive basis after consideration of their portfolio, grades in courses, and recommendation of faculty. The college also offers fine arts minor programs in arts administration, illustration, and art history. The program has a small affiliated art museum on the campus.

Crisp-Ellert Art Museum

This small museum on the Flagler College campus shows contemporary painting and sculpture, with exhibits, usually of the work of a single contemporary artist, changing periodically.

Plan your visit: Flagler College, 48 Sevilla Street, St. Augustine, (904) 826-8530.

GALLERIES: KING STREET GROUP

Phillip Anthony Signature Gallery

This small shop has a reputation for personal service, representing several local artists, who are often in the shop to meet potential customers.

Plan your visit: 9 King Street, St. Augustine, (904) 327-4080.

Cutter and Cutter Fine Art

The owners of this gallery also operate a framing shop as well as a secure warehouse and a shipping department, and another gallery in Ponte Vedra Beach. The shop offers original paintings and sculptures and limited edition prints.

Plan your visit: 25 King Street, St. Augustine, (904) 810-0460.

Grand Bohemian Gallery

Grand Bohemian Gallery, located on the King Street side of the Casa Monica Hotel, offers a selection of art ranging from oil paintings to wood and bronze sculptures, glass, contemporary jewelry, and unique gift items. Art on offer includes works by contemporary, internationally known artists, as well as a few artists local to St. Augustine. The gallery is one of several established by

hotelier and art enthusiast Richard C. Kessler. There are six elegant "Grand Bohemian" art galleries in the United States, including one in Orlando, Florida, all associated with luxury hotels. (See page 87 in Orlando entry.)

Plan your visit: 49 King Street, St. Augustine, (904) 829-6880.

Butterfield Garage Art Gallery

This "garage" gallery specializes in the work of well-known local artists, including Beau Redmond, Roxanne Horvath, Sydney McKenna, and Jan Miller.

Plan your visit: 137 West King Street, #B, St. Augustine, (904) 825-4577.

Lost Art Gallery

The director of this gallery is Victoria Golden, an accredited art appraiser. She has been involved in archaeological explorations in Central America, South America, and Indonesia and has been inducted into the exclusive organization the Explorers' Club. The shop offers prints and originals by internationally recognized contemporary artists as well as prints of Old Masters.

Plan your visit: 210 St. George Street, Suite C-1, St. Augustine, (904) 827-9800.

Plum Gallery

This bright, white-walled gallery displays art by contemporary painters and sculptors. The shop presents the work of some thirty-six contemporary artists, of whom twenty-eight are women. Prices are in the medium to high range.

Plan your visit: 10 Aviles Street, St. Augustine, (904) 825-0069.

Aviles Street Gallery

This gallery offers framed art by local painters and photographers, as well as jewelry.

Plan your visit: 11 Aviles Street, #C, St. Augustine, (904) 823-8608.

Trip Harrison Studio and Gallery

This studio/gallery offers original and limited edition fine art, as well as sculpture. Many of the framed paintings reflect seascapes and beach scenes.

Plan your visit: 22 Cathedral Place, St. Augustine, (904) 824-3662.

Grace Gallery

The Grace Gallery carries a wide variety of African masks.

Plan your visit: 82 Charlotte Street, St. Augustine, (904) 826-1668.

Old City Fine Art and More

Also known as Erbco Fine Art, the shop offers original art, at very affordable prices, and framing services as well.

Plan your visit: 9 Spanish Street, St. Augustine, (904) 829-1881.

GALLERIES: ANASTASIA ISLAND

High Tide Gallery

Located across the Bridge of Lions, on Anastasia Island, this shop has been nominated as the best gift shop on the island. The shop carries works by local artists and craftspeople.

Plan your visit: 850 Anastasia Boulevard, St. Augustine, (904) 315-6690.

ST. AUGUSTINE ART ASSOCIATION

Founded in 1924, the art association hosts monthly juried exhibits, exhibits by individual artists and groups, lectures and workshops for adults, and a variety of programs for children, as well as events such as concerts. The permanent collection includes some pieces by the founding members, some identified as among the "Lost Colony." The organization also produces the annual St. Augustine Art & Craft Festival at Francis Field and organizes a "Plein Air Paint Out," a "Tactile Show for the Blind," and the "Art y Facts of Drake's Raid" focused on presenting aspects of St. Augustine's history through art.

Plan your visit: 22 Marine Street, St. Augustine, (904) 824-2310.

NEW SMYRNA BEACH

Originally known as New Smyrna, the community grew around a plantation settlement about seventy miles to the south of St. Augustine, established in 1768 by Dr. Andrew Turnbull, a wealthy British doctor. He named the locale after the birthplace of his wife: Smyrna, a Greek town on the Mediterranean coast of what is present-day Turkey. Turnbull had an elaborate plan to establish a plantation to raise indigo, worked by white indentured servants in the colony of Florida, then held by Great Britain. He imported the workers from several points in the Mediterranean, including the island of Majorca, then a British-held island, now a part of Spain. Collectively, the indentured workers on his plantation became known as Majorcans.

Turnbull had enlisted the workers with the promise that after a few years of unpaid labor, they would be released—indentured servitude was a form of temporary slavery. However, his exploitation of the workers led to protests and their eventual abandonment of the plantation. The Majorcans who survived simply walked off in 1777, trudging the seventy miles north to settle in St. Augustine. The story of their recruitment, conditions in New Smyrna, and their overland march to St. Augustine is told in a small museum in St. Augustine, the St. Photios Shrine, at 41 St. George Street, and in our earlier volume, *St. Augustine in History*.

Turnbull's plantation fell into disrepair. Old Fort Park, two blocks north of Canal Street on the Indian River waterfront, is assumed to be a structure built by Dr. Turnbull's workers, although he never mentioned the site in his surviving writings about New Smyrna. In fact, Canal Street in downtown New Smyrna Beach, the location of several art galleries, is partially constructed over one of the canals built by Majorcan labor for Turnbull's plantation. Archaeologists for the National Park Service have determined that portions of the original canal are now buried underneath the sidewalk along the north side of Canal Street.

In 1947, the town leaders renamed the town as New Smyrna Beach, hoping to attract some of the growing number of northern tourists who flock to the Florida coast in the winter.

New Smyrna Beach has several features that evoke a sense of a "classic" art colony. There is an active community of artists, including many who are early in their careers; an art center that fosters accomplished artists, those earlier in their career, and amateurs as well; and several art galleries, some of which offer classes or studio space. The galleries and the large number of facilities offering classes of one kind or another in the arts generate a creative environment that competes with the "beach town" ambience.

GALLERIES: CANAL STREET NEIGHBORHOOD

The gallery scene in New Smyrna Beach is dynamic in that some galleries change hands or go out of business, while new shops join the group. Some of the galleries offer the work of the owner/artist, while others are devoted to specialties such as photography, framing, or ceramics. Many of the New Smyrna Beach galleries noted below in the year 2020 were clustered in two neighborhoods. One of these clusters, the Canal Street neighborhood, is the downtown section bounded by Orange Street on the west and Riverside Drive on the east, between Douglas and Canal Streets.

Studio Bleu

This facility offers classes and provides art studio space on a rental basis, with a focus on ceramics and pottery.

Plan your visit: 204 Magnolia Street, New Smyrna Beach, (386) 402-4966.

Clay Gallery

This gallery is in the home and the studio of Teresa Bowen; it features pottery work created there as well as the work of other local artists specializing in stained glass and painting.

Plan your visit: 302 South Riverside Drive, New Smyrna Beach, (386) 846-8203.

Jane's Art Center

This "eclectic fine art gallery" features both American and European artists and also offers ceramics workshops and classes.

Plan your visit: 199 Downing Street, New Smyrna Beach, (386) 402-8673.

Doris "Doc" Leeper

Doris Leeper (1929–2000) was both a sculptor and painter. Very active in community affairs, she worked to establish the Canaveral National Seashore in 1975 and founded the Atlantic Center for the Arts (ACA) in 1982, as well as Arts on Douglas in the 1990s in New Smyrna Beach. Born in 1929 in Charlotte, North Carolina, she attended Duke University, with the intention to become a brain surgeon. Although she changed her major to art history, graduating with a degree in that field in 1951, she earned the nickname "Doc" while in college for her early medical ambitions. After graduating, she worked in the commercial art field, and in 1958, she moved to the now-vanished community of Eldora, on the barrier island between New Smyrna Beach and Titusville.

By 1961, she had gained a national and international reputation as an artist, with works in some one hundred museum collections worldwide. With a range of styles, many of her works are geometric, highly colorful abstractions.

With the creation of the Canaveral National Seashore in 1975, her small town of Eldora was absorbed into the new preserve. She turned her social-activist energies to the creation of the Atlantic Center for the Arts in the mid-1970s, planning the artists' residency program there. After gaining support from friends and community leaders, she was able to win a challenge grant for $25,000 from the Rockefeller Foundation that was soon matched. With this and other funds that she raised, she was able to purchase the wooded property on the shore of Turnbull Bay. Over a period of eight years, a total of ten buildings were constructed, and an additional fifty-nine-acre area was purchased. The Atlantic Center for the Arts officially opened in 1982, and its first residency occupants were author James Dickey, sculptor Duane Hanson, and composer David Del Tredici. The program has continued, with several hundred master artists and more than thirty-five hundred associate artists over the years.

Leeper was awarded honorary doctorates from Duke University and Stetson University. She was named "Florida Ambassador of the Arts," and she was inducted into the Florida Artists Hall of Fame in 1999. She died April 11, 2000, still officially a resident of the small town of Eldora in the midst of the Canaveral National Seashore. The town no longer exists, and only two of its original buildings still stand.

The residency program at the ACA, Arts on Douglas, and the various community outreach programs hosted out of Harris House near the Arts on Douglas gallery in New Smyrna Beach are her living legacy.

Antiques and Art

A few blocks to the south of the Canal Street neighborhood is Antiques and Art, which sells clocks and other antiques and carries some works of the late twentieth-century African American artists "The Highwaymen." Many of the Highwaymen sold their works along this stretch of the Florida coast; collectors of the Highwaymen may find some hidden treasures in this eclectic shop. For more detail on the Highwaymen, see the discussion of the A. E. Backus Museum and Gallery in Fort Pierce on pages 52–53.

Plan your visit: 520 Andrews Street, New Smyrna Beach, (386) 427-9910.

Florida Galleria

This shop features local art, antiques, and works by the Florida Highwaymen.

Plan your visit: 427 Canal Street, New Smyrna Beach, (386) 427-7979.

GALLERIES: FLAGLER AVENUE

A second district in New Smyrna Beach, on the beach side of town, across the North Causeway from the downtown section, runs along Flagler Avenue. Among the many restaurants and souvenir, beachwear, and gift shops that cater to beach visitors, there are several shops selling art. Among them are these two galleries:

Jonah's Cat's Gallery

This gallery specializes in the work of Samuel Ruder, born 1949, whose whimsical works often feature wide-eyed cats in amusing poses.

Plan your visit: 220 Flagler Avenue, New Smyrna Beach, (513) 410-1438.

Ring Gallery

This gallery sells limited edition photography prints by the owner, Mike Ring.

Among the shops near the beach at New Smyrna Beach is Jonah's Cat's, owned by artist Samuel Ruder.

Plan your visit: 311 Flagler Avenue, New Smyrna Beach, (386) 427-1882.

ART CENTERS

Arts on Douglas

This gallery and art center focuses on the art of prominent Florida artists and is affiliated with the Atlantic Center for the Arts, operating in effect as the "museum shop" of the center, as explained to us by its long-term director, Meghan Martin. The gallery carries the work of some forty Florida artists.

Arts on Douglas first opened in 1991, founded by Doris Leeper, who had already established the Atlantic Center for the Arts in the early 1980s; she wanted to open a gallery for Florida artists. The building purchased on the corner of Douglas and Magnolia Streets was a former Ford car dealership. Doris Leeper and fellow artist Ed Harris had the building gutted and transformed into a modern commercial gallery building. The gallery was originally set up as a separate for-profit facility. Under the management of Meghan Martin, who has served with the organization since 1991, Arts on Douglas formalized its affiliation as a for-profit center with the Atlantic Center for the Arts in 2018, with a status like that of a museum shop.

The Arts on Douglas gallery, affiliated with the Atlantic Center for the Arts, offers art for sale. Here, a one-artist show presents works by Copper Tritscheller.

The nearby Harris House (on Riverside Drive) is also a division of the Atlantic Center for the Arts. It opened early in the 1990s when its original focus was to have a gallery downstairs and then to serve as the facility for a variety of community programs, such as an art camp, from the upstairs offices. The art camp moved into the Arts on Douglas building, where it continues as a thriving children's program, while the Harris House continues as an office for the various outreach programs of the organization.

Rather than defining New Smyrna Beach as an art colony, Ms. Martin commented that it might be called an "art-supporting community." A lot of the artists showing their work in Arts on Douglas live in Volusia County, but the gallery displays the works of artists from all over Florida. Like some of the other, smaller galleries in New Smyrna Beach, Arts on Douglas not only offers art for sale, but also maintains a robust offering of art classes in two large studio rooms associated with the gallery, on the east side of the building.

Plan your visit: 123 Douglas, New Smyrna Beach, (386) 428-1123.

The Hub on Canal

This art center offers classes and workspace to aspiring artists. Among the courses and workshops offered are classes in art, music, writing, languages, reading, and wellness. The art classes include introduction to oil painting, poured

In the heart of the Canal Street gallery district of New Smyrna Beach, this mural can be seen on the Magnolia Street side of the Hub on Canal Art Center.

acrylics, mixed media, jewelry making and design, basket weaving, film, and collage.

Plan your visit: 132 Canal Street, New Smyrna Beach, (386) 959-3924.

Atlantic Center for the Arts

Meghan Martin pointed out that the ACA, founded by Doris Leeper, has an "amazing campus," with five award-winning buildings including a black box theater and a dance studio. The multidisciplinary residency program attracts master artists in different disciplines. On a rotating basis, three groups of twelve artists live on the campus, where three senior artists mentor the junior ones, and mingle for three weeks. She said that the program's goal is to get all these creative people together, and it is rewarding to see how

that transfers into their creative lives. She found it interesting to try to track the mingling of the viewpoints of, for example, a composer and a dramatist after they leave the center, which is one of the goals of the residency program. Out of town in a wooded setting, the ACA program of putting accomplished master artists together with a group of younger aspiring artists is designed to replicate the stimulating environment of rural, secluded, and somewhat remote places like early-day classic art colonies that attracted both artists and writers.

The residency program at the ACA is the largest art residency program in Florida and continues to meet its goal of bringing in groups of artists to live together for a period of time. The aspiring artists associate with each other and with internationally known master artists, in a wide variety of fields, spanning not only the visual arts of painting and sculpture, but also photography, music, drama, film, video, multimedia, architecture, music (both composition and performance), literature, choreography, dance, performance art, and theater. The extensive campus provides not only housing but chef-prepared meals, as well as ample studio, rehearsal, and performance space for the artists.

The ACA also offers a wide range of classes, workshops, and outreach programs to the public, with a wide variety of goals. Some of the programs involve learning art skills, while others are designed to "relieve stress, build self-esteem, create positive shared experience, and strengthen social relationships," according to Nancy Norman, executive director at ACA.

Plan your visit: 1414 Art Center Avenue, New Smyrna Beach, (386) 427-6975.

The Atlantic Center for the Arts in New Smyrna Beach has an extensive campus, including a large display gallery and reception building at the entrance.

MELBOURNE/EAU GALLIE ARTS DISTRICT (EGAD)

The town of Melbourne is divided by the Eau Gallie River that flows to the Indian River (itself part of the Intracoastal Waterway that runs from Boston down the Atlantic coast to Miami and then continues around the Gulf of Mexico to Texas). The neighborhood of Eau Gallie, which was formerly a separate town founded in the 1850s, is a relatively small neighborhood on the north side of the Eau Gallie River. Although the name sounds French, "gallie" is not a French word; the name of the river is assumed to mean "rocky water."

An officially designated neighborhood since 2010, the Eau Gallie Arts District (EGAD) hosts the Foosaner Art Museum and a small shopping neighborhood that runs along Highland Avenue. In addition to the art museum, Highland Avenue has

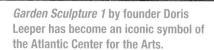

Garden Sculpture 1 by founder Doris Leeper has become an iconic symbol of the Atlantic Center for the Arts.

The Eau Gallie Arts District has numerous murals, including *Girl with Bird* by Christopher Martin.

several art galleries, a picture framing shop, and five of the district's twenty-two large outdoor murals found on the exterior walls of buildings.

The EGAD neighborhood organization is an affiliated member of the National Main Street Program. The Main Street America movement is devoted to reviving the urban centers of small towns in the United States. Based in Chicago and formed in the 1980s, this organization, a subsidiary of the National Trust for Historic Preservation, works with the business and government leaders of small towns to revive neighborhoods by helping to arrange funding and planning through "preservation-based economic development." The emphasis is on attracting businesses, documenting the historical nature of older central business districts, and increasing both tourism and local shopping. By 2020, more than sixteen hundred communities have participated. Although not focused on towns with art colony reputations, many of the main street communities have attempted to attract artists and craftspeople as part of the economic stimulus. In Florida, both Eau Gallie and Melbourne have

participated in the Main Street America program, as has Fernandina.

A statement issued by the local Main Street organization of the Eau Gallie Arts District emphasizes the district's heritage as a separate town and consciously stresses art as a stimulus for revitalization of a neighborhood: "EGAD Main Street uses arts as a catalyst towards our goal of renewal—from crafting coffee, beer, or food to architectural, hair and flower design—we are the epicenter of authenticity on the Space Coast."

Throughout the EGAD neighborhood, hanging flags identify the neighborhood, while small blue-and-white glass-encased placards provide historical details of Eau Gallie as a separate town. For example, one such placard near the corner of Highland Avenue and St. Clair Street describes the arrival of the Florida East Coast Railway, built by Henry Flagler, in the community on May 20, 1893. While the line was being pushed on toward Miami, Eau Gallie was the temporary southern terminus of the railway. A spur line connected the main line to a point on the Indian River, near the present location

Bauhaus and Bauhaus Movement

One of the collections at the Foosaner documents the Bauhaus influence in design. The Bauhaus was an art and design school in Germany that operated in the years 1919–1933, led by Walter Gropius. The emphasis was on a new concept of design, in which "form follows function." That is, Gropius and his coworkers argued that the design of buildings, furnishings, and appliances should not involve extraneous decoration, but should consist of plain, undecorated surfaces and clean lines, derived directly from the function of the object and from the nature of its materials. Buildings were designed with very boxy and rectangular lines; household furniture and appliances were similarly stripped of any extraneous, unnecessary decorative elements. The result was a clean, sharp image in which lines of the device or structure were set by the potential of the materials themselves, such as metal, leather, or plastic, and the purpose of the device or structure; the concept soon defined the new and distinctly "modern" look. The movement affected not only architecture over the next century, but also design of hundreds of familiar utensils, appliances, and furniture. While the Bauhaus school was closed under the Nazi regime, Walter Gropius moved to the United States where he taught at Harvard from 1937 to 1952, and the ideas of the movement continued to influence design. Another Bauhaus instructor, Joseph Albers, taught for fifteen years at Black Mountain College in North Carolina, and then at Yale University. In Florida, the premier collection of household appliances designed by Bauhaus-influenced designer Walter von Nessen is found at the Foosaner Museum in the Eau Gallie district of Melbourne.

of the Eau Gallie Library on Pineapple Avenue. For a period of three years, cargo was transferred across the Indian River, creating a local land boom in the 1890s.

MUSEUMS

Foosaner Art Museum
In addition to the galleries and shops in both Eau Gallie and downtown Melbourne, the community hosts this large and thriving art museum.

Since its opening as the Brevard Art Center and Museum in 1978, the museum has amassed a collection of some five thousand objects. The permanent collection focuses on modern and contemporary art. Two unique groups are the Conill-Mendoza Collection of American Industrial Design and a definitive collection of works by the

German impressionist artist Ernst Oppler (1867–1929).

Enrique Conill-Mendoza, a Cuban-born collector of modern design, became fascinated with the Bauhaus-influenced design of such items as lamps, doorstops, and other household devices, especially those of the Chase Brass and Copper Company designed by Walter von Nessen (1889–1945).

Walter von Nessen designed numerous household appliances, now highly valued as examples of pioneering "modern," functional art. Conill-Mendoza laboriously put together a collection of more than one thousand such items that represented the merger of design and utility in home appliances, lamps, and fixtures. He later donated a portion of his collection to the Brevard Art Center and Museum, now

The Foosaner Museum displays this sculpture on the exterior titled *Hot Rods II*, donated by the artist, George Snyder.

the Foosaner. Documenting the lasting influence of 1920s German modernism on the design of home appliances and furnishings, the Foosaner collection assembled by Conill Mendoza is unique, important, and informative.

The other unique collection of the Foosaner Museum is the group of works by Ernst Oppler. Oppler was regarded in the 1920s as one of the most prominent members of the German avant-garde and maintained a studio in Berlin, together

with his brother, a sculptor. Among his works were many documenting the history of the ballet in Germany. The Foosaner is one of very few museums in the United States with collections of Oppler's works.

The first building of the Foosaner Museum was originally the city hall of the separate town of Eau Gallie. It was modified to create a forty-five-hundred-square-foot exhibition space consisting of three galleries. Cocoa

Beach philanthropist Samuel J. Foosaner provided a major financial gift in 1980, allowing for the purchase of an additional six-thousand-square-foot building next door. That building was remodeled to host a program of studio classes for both children and adults, in the Renee Foosaner Education Center. In a further expansion in 1986, the museum acquired a five-gallery space across Highland Avenue, providing space for more

The Foosaner Museum holds a definitive collection of Bauhaus-influenced household appliances and hosts annual Florida artist shows.

exhibitions, offices, and storage. As of late 2020, planners were considering moving the Foosaner collection to another location, possibly to the campus of the Florida Institute of Technology in Melbourne, so those visitors planning a trip to the museum should check its current status and location.

Plan your visit: 1463 Highland Avenue, Eau Gallie, (321) 674-8916.

GALLERIES

Fifth Avenue Art Gallery

This gallery is cooperatively owned and operated, featuring the works of the eighteen participating artists. Established in 1974–1975, it is the oldest gallery in the area, showing works ranging from moderately priced wall art and sculpture to creations at the higher price range. Sue Tully, a member artist who was managing the gallery the day we visited, noted that the number of galleries in Eau Gallie has declined in recent years, but that the cooperative Fifth Avenue Art Gallery continues to thrive, with a wide range of wall art, sculpture, and ceramics, priced in the medium to upper ranges.

The gallery's website expresses the rationale and ethos of a cooperative art gallery very well:

> Every member artist is involved in the day to day operation of the gallery from press, marketing, hanging, to painting, replacing bulbs, gardening, dusting, cleaning—you name it we do it all. What makes this gallery look so attractive is the hard work, creativity

and elbow grease of every member. Active participation by all members is essential to the success of our gallery. Members are also responsible for working in the gallery a couple of days a month. They handle inquiries, sales transactions, and basic daily tasks.

For these reasons any customer or even a casual visitor who stops in to the gallery to make a purchase or to look at the works displayed is bound to encounter one of the participating artists and an enthusiastic and informative advocate of the arts and of the gallery itself.

Plan your visit: 1470 Highland Avenue, Eau Gallie, (321) 537-4220.

A block to the south on Highland Avenue from the Fifth Avenue Art Gallery in Eau Gallie is a small alley, flanked on each side by an art gallery, with a work-shop-studio available for walk-in aspiring artists at the back of the alley.

Shambala Boutique

On the right-hand side of the alley, Shambala Boutique sells an eclectic mix of art and collectibles, with many items produced by local artists.

Plan your visit: 1419 Highland Avenue, Eau Gallie, (321) 508-5351.

Eau Gallery

Across the entrance to the alley, Eau Gallery sells "original art and hand-crafted gifts." The shop was established in 2004 as the Art and Antique Gallery by local artist and watercolor teacher Theresa Ferguson and antiques specialist Debbie McElwain. In February 2019, the artists showing in the gallery reorganized the

Peonies by member artist Sue Tully, on display at the Fifth Avenue Art Gallery in Eau Gallie. *Photographed by Loretta Carlisle with permission of the artist*

shop as Eau Gallery. Now a cooperative gallery, the shop represents the works of some fifteen local member-artists. In addition to the co-op members, the gallery accepts works on consignment from other artists, and features a "2D or 3D" artist (i.e., works by an artist making two-dimensional wall art, or three-dimensional sculpture or ceramics) each month with a show in the main room.

Information about "First Friday evening" gallery walking tours is available at the Shambala Boutique or at the Eau Gallery.

Plan your visit: 1429 Highland Avenue, Eau Gallie, (321) 253-5533.

Derek Gores

This shop features collages and mixed media works by the owner, Derek Gores.

Plan your visit: 587 West Eau Gallie Avenue, Eau Gallie, (321) 258-2119.

Besides art galleries, the Eau Gallie Arts District has several other kinds of art-related shops and stores that include an antique revamping shop, a busy art supply store, and jewelry and gift shops.

MELBOURNE

South of the Eau Gallie Arts District, across the Eau Gallie River, is the main section of the town of Melbourne that hosts an active shopping district that runs along New Haven Avenue. The community organizes several activities that draw shoppers, including several that focus on the arts. These include a monthly "Friday Fest" that brings crowds to all the shops, two yearly art shows, and a monthly art walk. Other festivals bring in thousands of visitors, and the various galleries in both downtown Melbourne and in Eau Gallie benefit from these visitors.

GALLERIES

Strawbridge Art League

Just to the north of the "main street" of New Haven Avenue is Strawbridge Avenue, a neighborhood that includes the Strawbridge Art League Gallery at 819 Strawbridge Avenue. The organization, founded in 1997, accepts new members and included more than 140 artists in the year 2020. The league holds ten to fifteen shows annually and actively cooperates with a number of local charities and organizations including the SPCA, the

Lions Club, Walk for Life, the Wildlife Hospital, and others.

Plan your visit: 819 East Strawbridge Avenue, Melbourne, (321) 952-3070.

Creative Bazaar

Down the "La Galerie" alley at number five, Creative Bazaar sells a variety of gifts, "creative totes," and other locally handmade unique items.

Plan your visit: 819 East Strawbridge Avenue, Melbourne, (321) 301-0158.

Living Room Art Gallery and Wine Lounge

This unique gallery offers a wine bar, musical entertainment, and food service, as well as showing art for sale.

Plan your visit: 2018 Melbourne Court, Melbourne, (321) 345-4395.

Painting with a Twist studio

At the corner of New Haven Avenue and Livingston Avenue, Painting with a Twist is organized along the same lines as the shop by the same name in Mount Dora and elsewhere, where local artists and aspiring artists gather in the evenings to paint and "bring their own bottle" of wine.

Plan your visit: 702 East New Haven Avenue, Melbourne, (321) 698-7928.

FORT PIERCE

MUSEUMS

A. E. Backus Museum and Gallery/ The Highwaymen

This museum is devoted to the work of a single artist, A. E. Backus (1906–1990), who was born and grew up in Fort Pierce. He had little formal training, studying two summers (1924–1925) at the Parsons

School in New York City. That school had been established in 1896 in the Greenwich Village neighborhood of the city and represented a break with the established Art Students League of New York. Later, under the direction of Frank Alvah Parsons, the school became renowned for its commitment to a democratized taste in design. Decades after Backus attended, the Parsons School became affiliated with New York's School for Social Research.

Backus worked as a sign painter and painted some theater marquees before being encouraged to take up serious landscape painting. His work has been compared to the Romantic landscapes of the early nineteenth-century Hudson River school, which depicted the then frontier of upstate New York in bold and colorful paintings that romanticized the "wilderness" along the Hudson River in New York State. Backus's influence on painters and his Romantic depiction of Florida scenes have sometimes been identified as the "Indian River school" of painting, echoing the Hudson River name.

Backus worked at first in bold strokes with a palette knife, later refining his technique with brush, painting scenes from the Florida backwoods and the Everglades.

Although Backus is credited as influencing the African American painters known as the Highwaymen, he apparently only taught one of them, Al Hair, quite briefly. However, many of the group of twenty-six painters, one of whom was a woman, clearly emulated his style as they produced hundreds, and later thousands, of pieces of work in the mid-1930s into the post–World War II years.

The Highwaymen earned their reputation and nickname for their practice of quickly painting landscapes in their homes or garages, then loading them in their cars to sell to motels, cafes, and individual buyers along the coast of Florida from Highway 1 and, later, from I-95. Using palette knives and broad brushes, and usually painting on inexpensive Upson board (an inexpensive laminated fiberboard) rather than canvas, the Highwaymen conveyed an idealized and brightly colored vision of Florida wilderness, beach scenes, and simple backwoods structures. Many of their romanticized scenes reflected themes and even subject matter of particular paintings that Backus had created. He knew of their work and encouraged it, asking only that they did not sell it in Fort Pierce as buyers might think they were acquiring one of his own paintings.

The African American Highwaymen, working in the years from the 1930s into the 1960s and later, were not usually able to find galleries that would show their works because of racial discrimination, and that accounted for their unusual method of direct sales. Many of them would paint several pictures at the same time, of a single scene, increasing their output far beyond what was typical of artists in the period. They usually sold their paintings for prices in the range of $25–$35, earning far more per week in those decades of discrimination in employment than they could hope to make in the available jobs. Unannounced, they would stop at motels, cafés, and offices and knock on doors, offering their works, often clearing out the trunk of their car in a day.

Florida Highwaymen

Curtis Arnett
Hezekiah Baker
Al Black
Ellis Buckner
George Buckner
Robert Butler
Mary Ann Carroll (the only woman "Highwayman")
Johnnie Daniels
Willie Daniels
Rodney Demps
James Gibson
Alfred Hair
Issac Knight
Robert L. Lewis
John Maynor
Roy McLendon
Alfonso Moran
Harold Newton
Lemuel Newton
Sam Newton
Willie Reagan
Livingston Roberts
Carnell (Pete) Smith
Charles Walker
Sylvester M. Wells
Charles Wheeler

Today, authenticated works by the Highwaymen ordinarily sell in the $250–$400 range, with some of the larger and best pieces priced much higher. Most of the artists signed their works, but some unsigned pieces have been authenticated. Collectors and buyers have become concerned in recent years that forgeries or frauds have popped up, so getting a painting authenticated as a genuine "Highwayman" has become important to collectors.

Many of the paintings followed themes established by Backus or by one of the Highwaymen—such as scenes of moonlight over bay waters, palm trees framing a water scene with a very few gliding birds, or paintings of a royal poinciana tree, with vivid, orange-red blossoms against a background of palms and a bay inlet. Most of the painters did not include figures of people in their landscapes, and many repeated their subjects, themes, and even specific scenes over and over.

Al Hair, the only one of the Highwaymen to have studied directly under Backus, was killed in a barroom fight in 1970, and the production of works by most of the group declined in the following years. The name "Highwaymen" became attached to the group in the 1990s after a series of articles by Florida art historian Jim Fitch and other articles by Jeff Klinkenberg of the *St. Petersburg Times*. After that revival of interest in their work, surviving members of the Highwaymen resumed painting in the early twenty-first century. Estimates of the total number of works produced by the twenty-six artists have run as high as two hundred thousand paintings, although no exact count has been established.

In addition to the display at the Backus Museum in Fort Pierce, shows of their works have been mounted in museums and other venues from time to time, such as an annual presentation in Mount Dora.

Plan your visit: 500 North Indian River Drive, Fort Pierce, (772) 465-0630.

Samuel P. Harn Museum.

GAINESVILLE

MUSEUMS

Harn Museum of Art

The museum's curators have worked to assemble a collection that covers the sweep of art of a variety of periods and cultures, serving as supplements to art history courses, as inspiration to art students, and as a cultural addition to the community. The museum's collection of more than ten thousand items includes African, Asian, modern, and contemporary art, along with ancient American and oceanic art. The museum is expanding its collection of prints and drawings created prior to 1850. The modern (1850–1950) and contemporary (1950–present) parts of the collection total more than twenty-five hundred pieces.

A major strength of the modern collection is its representation of American art, including landscapes, urban and social realist themes, and prints from the Franklin Roosevelt era, Works Progress Administration (WPA) prints. These works, together with the collection of Latin American art, reflect a wide variety of twentieth- and twenty-first-century movements, ranging from impressionism through social realism, to abstract works. The variety of styles and periods provides material not only for the study by students at the university, but also a wide selection in an effort to meet the varied interests of the general public visiting the museum.

An example of the interesting smaller historical displays is that of the Park Avenue Cubists, so-called because the four painters were relatively affluent in contrast to many artists of the era. This group of paintings is rather unusual in that it tells a story of a group of artists who did not quite "fit the mold" in other ways in the 1920s and 1930s. The four artists had traveled extensively in Europe, where they had absorbed ideas of Pablo Picasso and Georges Braque, among others. The four painters were Albert Gallatin, Charles G. Shaw, and a married couple: George Morris and Suzy Frelinghuysen. They had exhibited together in the annual show of the American Abstract Artists that had been founded in 1936. However, in the atmosphere of the mid- and late 1930s, in which social realism or paintings reflecting the plight and strengths of the poor and the working class were popular, the abstract work of cubists and other abstract painters like these four received little support in the United States. Furthermore, the painters' relatively prosperous financial status did not conform to the notion of "struggling" artists, leading to the group's ironic nickname.

The museum's Contemporary Collection includes some fifteen hundred objects (paintings, sculptures, and other media) from all over the world, and selections from that collection are displayed in the Mary Ann Harn Cofrin Pavilion and the outside Bob and Nancy Magoon Garden. As in many other museums, specific show spaces and galleries are named for generous supporters whose donations helped fund expansion of facilities or purchases of art.

Plan your visit: University of Florida, 3259 Hull Road, Gainesville, (352) 392-9826.

University of Florida, Gainesville

The University of Florida at Gainesville offers a wide range of degrees in art, including a BA, BFA, and MFA in studio art, as well as bachelor's and higher degrees: MA in art education; BA, MA, and PhD in art history; BFA in graphic design; MFA in design and visual communication; and MA in museum studies. The Harn Museum, operated by the university, is a major art museum serving central Florida.

GALLERIES

There are several picture framing shops and a number of shops selling crafts and gifts in Gainesville that are often listed as "galleries" but do not in fact specialize in original art. In addition, there is both a local artisans' guild gallery, which represents a large community of local artists and craft workers, as well as a historical art center. The following art galleries were in business in early 2020:

WARPhaus Gallery
This gallery is linked to the University of Florida Art Department.

Plan your visit: 534 SW Fourth Avenue, Gainesville, (352) 226-8217.

Paddiwhack

This shop has a reputation for "shabby chic" items.

Plan your visit: 1510 NW Thirteenth Street, Gainesville, (352) 336-3175.

Eleanor Blair Studio

This gallery sells prints, reproductions, and old posters, as well as Eleanor Blair's own Florida landscape paintings in oil.

Plan your visit: 113 South Main Street, Gainesville, (352) 316-1751.

Gainesville Artisans' Guild Gallery

This local artists' cooperative was established in 1970, and in early 2020 listed about fifty active members. This cooperative gallery is the major outlet for original art in the city. The member artists work in a wide variety of media, with eleven specializing in jewelry; nine in textiles and leather; eight in painting; eight in mixed media; and smaller numbers in pottery, printmaking, glass, photography, and woodworking.

Plan your visit: 201 SE Second Place, Gainesville, (352) 378-1383.

ART CENTER

Thomas Center

This large former private residence and hotel is now a cultural events center, serving Gainesville and nearby communities. The building is frequently used as a wedding venue and for other events, including art exhibits.

Plan your visit: 302 NE Sixth Avenue, Gainesville, (352) 393-8539.

OCALA

MUSEUMS

Appleton Museum of Art

This large and very elegant art museum on the eastern edge of Ocala opened in 1987. The museum has been affiliated with the College of Central Florida since 2004 and is in an "arts complex" that also includes a theater for the performing arts. Designed by Tampa architect Dwight Holmes, the exterior of the museum is clad in brilliant marble and is faced by a long reflecting pool. The interior is arranged on two stories that surround a large rectangular center courtyard; its galleries house a permanent collection of more than eighteen thousand objects. Many of the items are the legacy of the personal collection of Arthur I. Appleton, supplemented by later donations and purchases. Recent purchases have included works by Pablo Picasso and Alexander Calder, among others.

In the museum's auditorium, an exhibit of illustrations and informative panels gives the background of the Appleton family, whose fortune derived from Albert Ivar Appleton, the founder of an electrical supply company in 1905. His son, Arthur I. Appleton, was born in 1915. Arthur developed a fascination in the arts as a child, influenced by his mother who was herself a collector of fine art. Arthur Appleton received a master's degree in business from Dartmouth in 1936, served in the navy in World War II, and became a prolific inventor as well as executive of the Appleton firm. In 1982, he retired from the business and sold it to Emerson Electric. He and his wife, the cinema actress Martha O'Driscoll, bought land near Ocala and set up Bridlewood Farm, a thorough-bred horse breeding and training facility. Over his life, he and his wife accumulated a vast collection of art, which forms the core of the exhibits at the museum.

One room is devoted to a collection of African art, donated from the estate of Victor David DuBois, a prolific scholar who died at the relatively young age of fifty-one. DuBois was an avid and careful collector of pieces from Mali, Nigeria, and Upper Volta while he was working in West Africa on a study of contemporary political

This impressive reflecting pond and marble façade of the Appleton Museum of Art in Ocala welcomes visitors.

issues. The pieces were well documented by DuBois and were mostly collected during his visits in the early 1960s.

Among the other permanent collections of the Appleton are a collection of antique clocks and selections of pre-Columbian art, Asian art, and "Orientalist art." "Orientalist" describes paintings produced in the late nineteenth and early twentieth centuries by Western (i.e., European and American) artists who presented images of life in the Middle East and Far East. The paintings were essentially fantasy portrayals of an exotic East, with features such as veiled women, harem scenes, and other imagined settings, drawn from

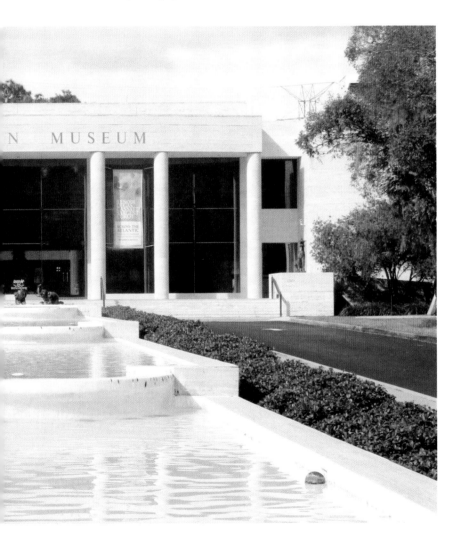

a romanticized interpretation of life in North Africa and the Middle East.

Other exhibits of fine art include works from the Romantic period of nineteenth-century European painting, as well as the more realistic Barbizon school. That term refers to an art group that emphasized realism, often showing humble people in their natural settings, a reaction against the more dominant Romantic style of the period through the mid-1800s in Europe.

In addition to the displays in the museum, the Appleton has an extensive program of one-day workshops, and multiday classes and programs for adults and families. These include classes in watercolor, in working with clay, in fabric, and in "wearable canvas." Family activities include

Charioteer by Antonio Vanetti.

programs such as drawing sketches of objects or paintings in the galleries, youth classes in painting and drawing, and teen classes in ceramics, glass fusing, and clay.

Plan your visit: Appleton Museum, College of Central Florida, 4333 East Silver Springs Boulevard, Ocala, (352) 291-4455.

WINTER PARK

The small town of Winter Park (population about twenty-five to thirty thousand) is just seven miles north of downtown Orlando and is now largely suburban in nature, with several shopping districts. It was founded in the 1880s as a resort community with lakefronts on Lake Osceola, Lake Virginia, and Lake Killarney. Over the years, Winter Park has developed several institutions devoted to the arts. At present, the town hosts three fine arts museums, an annual outdoor painting contest, and an annual juried sidewalk art festival that has been in operation for sixty years, as well as a school of art that maintains a museum-style show space. Numerous large homes designed by noted architects add to the community's charm and attraction. The three museums in this small community are among the major cultural attractions in central Florida. These art museums, the art school, the annual arts events, and art galleries all attest to the town's continuing reputation as an art destination.

As land values for both commercial and residential properties have increased, few self-supporting, beginning artists can afford to live and work directly in Winter Park. The median value of a private home in Winter Park climbed from just over $200,000 in 2012 to over $400,000 in 2019. The decline of Winter Park as an art colony is reflected in the April 2016 closing of McRae Art Studios, a collective, shared warehouse space on Railroad Avenue. That closure displaced some twenty-three artists' studios from a ten-thousand-square-foot space in Winter Park. The warehouse was listed for sale at a reputed $1.3 million. The collective had shared space in the warehouse for eighteen years, holding one or two shows per year. The closing led to the relocation of the McRae Art Studios and workshops to a new location within the Orlando city limits, at 1000 Arlington Street, about five miles to the south of the center of Winter Park. The move of the McRae Art Studios to the less costly space outside of Winter Park is a very clear and specific example of the ways in which the increase of real estate values in towns or urban districts once thought of as art colonies has often resulted in a diminished presence of beginning or midcareer artists.

Civitas by Audrey Flack greets visitors in the Cornell Fine Arts Museum on the campus of Rollins College in Winter Park.

MUSEUMS

George D. and Harriet W. Cornell Fine Arts Museum at Rollins College

Located on Lake Virginia, Cornell Fine Arts Museum shows antiquities and contemporary works. This museum offers guided tours by arrangement for groups of eight or more. This art museum has a large collection, spanning work from ancient times to the present, with more than fifty-six hundred works, including more than seven hundred paintings; two thousand prints, photographs, and drawings; and sculpture and archaeological artifacts. The museum offers major works from European, American, and contemporary art, ranging from the 1400s to the

Resting, a 1944 work by Claude Clark, an African American artist who had studied at the Barnes Foundation in Philadelphia, is on display at the Cornell Fine Arts Museum on the campus of Rollins College in Winter Park.

present time. Admission is free, which is quite rare in the present era.

Exhibits are changed periodically, as in many art museums. Recent exhibits have included work by African American artists and a gallery devoted to Walt Whitman. Items from the permanent collection have included "images of repose" by European and American painters from the seventeenth through the early twentieth century. An ongoing exhibit is *The Place as Metaphor*, which includes literal works depicting cities, as well as symbolic places. The recent acquisition of more than seven hundred new works of art has led to periodic changes and placing pieces on loan from other collections "in conversation" with items from the permanent collection. An adjunct to the museum can be seen at the Alfond Inn at Rollins College campus—the Alfond Collection of Contemporary Art. In addition, a small sculpture garden is located around in back of the Cornell Fine Arts Museum.

Plan your visit: 1000 Holt Avenue, Winter Park, (407) 646-2526.

Charles Hosmer Morse Museum of American Art
One of Florida's leading cultural attractions, the Morse Museum presents the most thorough and documented collection of art glass, lamps, jewelry, and other art by Louis Comfort Tiffany (1848–1933). Among the unique displays is the Tiffany-designed, Tiffany-built chapel interior from the 1893 World's Fair in Chicago, a stunning and memorable masterpiece of stained glass art. Also included are pieces of art

and architectural details from Tiffany's home, Laurelton Hall, on Long Island, New York. Other pieces include late nineteenth- and early twentieth-century American paintings and decorative art. The museum advises visitors to allow at least ninety minutes to tour the collection. Admission is charged at a very modest rate for this quality of exhibit.

The story of the chapel is told in a short video presentation. After the 1893 World's Fair, the collection was housed in New York's Church of St. John the Divine, until a new architect took over the remodeling of the church and halted work on its preservation. The chapel had been virtually abandoned in the church in 1908, until Tiffany himself had it moved to his home on Long Island in 1916, where he restored the missing cross and did other repairs. After Tiffany's death in 1933, most of the contents of his home of Laurelton were sold off; his home itself was gutted by fire in 1957. After the fire, one of Tiffany's daughters contacted the president of Rollins College in Winter Park, Hugh McKean. He and his wife, Jeannette Genius McKean, had hosted a Tiffany exhibit in a museum dedicated to her father, Charles Hosmer Morse. Together the McKeans purchased the remains of the chapel and undertook the laborious process of gathering the damaged work and having it transported to Florida for restoration. There, museum staff conservators carefully cleaned the many pieces and then reassembled and stabilized the chapel. Among the treasures preserved was the spherical baptismal font as well as the altar, now on display at the Morse Museum. With

This baptismal font by Louis Comfort Tiffany is part of the restored Tiffany master-piece chapel from the 1893 Chicago World's Fair on display at the Morse Museum in Winter Park.

the gathering of other Tiffany objects, and the construction of the new museum on North Park Avenue, the museum now has the most comprehensive collection of Tiffany works anywhere in the world.

Among the many Tiffany lamps on display in gallery number "X" is item #146, a "cobweb" design, identical to one owned by Barbra Streisand; another, a floor lamp, is identical to one owned by Steve Jobs. Recent sales of such lamps have been at prices ranging up to $2.8 million. The museum also includes a number of separate galleries showing

Tiffany lamps at the Morse Museum, Winter Park.

This unusual Tiffany lamp is among the many masterpieces on display at the Morse Museum.

American paintings done between 1850 and 1909. Other displays include vases and furniture and a complete fireplace mantle, from the American Arts and Crafts movement of the early twentieth century. Other objects from the period include vases, lamps, and candlesticks from the art nouveau movement in Europe and America, and a display of the various buildings and art from Tiffany's estate of Laurelton Hall.

Every spring, the museum offers a series of Wednesday free afternoon lectures on topics related to Tiffany or to the arts of the Arts and Crafts or art nouveau movements, presented by visiting experts from around the United States. Other scheduled free events throughout the year include a series of free Friday films on art and architecture, art talks by visiting experts, and musical performances and evening tours.

Check with the museum for program specifics.

Plan your visit: 445 North Park Avenue, Winter Park, (407) 645-5311.

Albin Polasek Museum & Sculpture Gardens

The museum and gardens are located on Osceola Lake and display works by the noted Czech-American artist Albin Polasek (1879–1965). The museum was founded in 1961 and presents Polasek's life work of sculpture. Born in Moravia (now part of the Czech Republic), Albin Polasek moved to the United States in 1901 and began work as a wood carver. As his work attracted notice, he attended the Pennsylvania Academy of the Fine Arts in Philadelphia; he later studied at the American Academy in Rome. After gaining national fame, he served for twenty-seven years as chair of the Department of Sculpture at the Art Institute of Chicago. On retirement, he moved to Winter Park in 1950, residing in this large Mediterranean-style home overlooking the lake. Polasek first opened his home, studio, and gardens to the public in 1961. The museum is now supported by the Albin Polasek Foundation.

The museum holds a permanent collection of about two hundred pieces, made up of Polasek sculptures; some by his wife, Ruth Sherwood; and several items from the Polaseks' own collection

Pilgrim **by Albin Polasek in the sculpture garden at the Polasek Museum in Winter Park.**

Forest Idol by Albin Polasek.

Risen Christ by Albin Polasek, in the sculpture garden behind the Polasek home in Winter Park.

Wasserman, King under the Sea by Albin Polasek. A jovial mythological figure presides over a pond in the Polasek sculpture garden.

of antiquities. In addition, the galleries in the museum host exhibitions of work by local artists, some of which are for sale. The grounds include a butterfly garden and sculptures, as well as plantings and two water gardens.

In recent years, another historic home, the Capen-Showalter House, was relocated to the grounds of the Polasek Museum. This building includes museum offices as well as art exhibits, classrooms, and meeting rooms.

Among events scheduled by the museum is an annual "Winter Park Paint-Out" held in April. In this unique event, twenty-five artists complete artwork in the open

around the town of Winter Park over the period of a week, and the resulting works are then offered for sale at the museum.

Plan your visit: 633 Osceola Avenue, Winter Park, (407) 647-6294.

GALLERIES

Crealdé School of Art

Opened in 1975, the Crealdé School of Art is a nonprofit, community-supported school that offers classes in pictorial and three-dimensional art for a range of age groups. Classes include ceramics and pottery as well as drawing and painting. The school supports a summer art camp and a visiting artist program and has two separate galleries:

Alice and William Jenkins Gallery
Established in 1980, this museum-style gallery is operated by the Crealdé School of Art and is located on the campus of the school. Annual exhibitions are formally curated by a member of the Crealdé staff and focus on works by Florida artists.

Showalter Hughes Community Gallery
Established in the year 2000, this gallery presents four or five exhibitions each year. The shows feature work by students, faculty, and the school's outreach programs. The gallery provides seating for up to eighty for lectures and presentations by artists. In addition, the school maintains a sculpture garden.

Plan your visit: Crealdé School of Art, 600 St. Andrews Boulevard, Winter Park, (407) 671-1886.

In addition to several small galleries located in the single-artist settings of home and studio, locals and visitors support the following galleries, some of them clustered in the flourishing shopping district along North and South Park Avenue, anchored by the Morse Museum described above. Although dozens of shops along Park Avenue offer gifts, clothing, and items of décor, and numerous exotic small restaurants line the street, there are only two galleries directly on Park Avenue.

Ocean Blue Galleries
This gallery is the second one owned by three partners, following on an earlier shop in St. Petersburg. The gallery features contemporary original art and sculpture, much of it reflecting seascapes and marine life. Among the artists featured is the actor and come-dian Jim Carrey. Many of the ceramic, aluminum, and glass sculptures and wall art capture the iridescent quality of undersea life, reflected in the gallery's name.

Plan your visit: 202 North Park Avenue, Winter Park, (321) 295-7317.

Scott Laurent Collection
This shop sells a wide variety of lamps, sculpture, jewelry, vases, and other decorative pieces as well as framed art and has been in business for more than twenty-five years. Owner Rick Stanley notes that the gallery collection is "affordably priced."

Plan your visit: 348 North Park Avenue, Winter Park, (407) 629-0276.

Fine Arts Limited
Located off South Park Avenue. Owned by Mike Kuschmann, this gallery has been in business for more than twenty years and deals in original contemporary art at the high end of the price range

Plan your visit: 174 West Comstock Avenue, #101, Winter Park, (407) 702-6638.

Baterbys Art Gallery
This large gallery sells a wide variety of prints and original art and offers framing services as well.

Plan your visit: 925 Semoran Boulevard, #122, Winter Park, (888) 682-9995.

Mark Pulliam Fine Art
This artist-owned studio offers the original work of Mark Pulliam. Some of the works are available in prints. This gallery is open by appointment only.

Plan your visit: 897 South Orlando Avenue, Suite N, Winter Park, (407) 636 -9286.

Winter Park Sidewalk Art Festival
The Winter Park Sidewalk Art Festival is a large juried outdoor art festival that has been held since 1960. In recent years, more than a thousand artists have applied for participation; judges then narrow the presenters down to fewer than three hundred, all of them artists of national or international repute. An all-volunteer board of directors runs the annual festival, usually held in the third week of March. The festival is headquartered in the Morse Museum, described above. During the festival the Morse Museum is usually open to the public without admission charge.

ARCHITECTURE AS ART

James Gamble Rogers II, the son of the architect who designed the Gothic-style towers at Yale University, resided in Winter Park and designed several large Mediterranean-style homes and other buildings in the town. One is the Casa Feliz, which was moved to its present location to save it from destruction. It now serves as a wedding venue and community center. The building was designed to look old, using recycled bricks, and modeled on the floor plan of an Andalusian farmhouse with an inner courtyard. Tours are available.

Plan your visit: Casa Feliz, 656 North Park Avenue, Winter Park, (407) 628-8200.

Built to replicate a Spanish farmhouse, Casa Feliz is one of several architectural treasures in Winter Park.

MAITLAND
MAITLAND ART CENTER

The Maitland Art Center today offers one- to three-day workshops in a variety of arts including fiber art, jewelry, painting, pottery, and sculpture. In addition, the center offers a selection of classes that typically run for six or nine weeks, in topics such as sculpting, drawing, painting, and pottery. The goal is to offer "small, approachable class sizes for all skill levels." Studios on the grounds are rented to local central Florida artists, and one residency studio

Entrance to the Maitland Art Center.

is awarded on three-, six-, and nine-week bases to visiting artists.

However, for the visitor, the most interesting aspects of the Maitland Art Center are its very unusual design and the history of how it was funded and

founded. The buildings are designed in "Mayan Revival" style, a rare genre of architecture that is represented by a few examples built in the 1930s, influenced by the Mediterranean Revival. The structures, friezes, statuary, and design of the buildings show a blending of Central American, Christian, Hispanic, and twentieth-century "modern" themes that is quite unique.

A modest fee is charged for admission to the museum and gallery portion of the center, while the grounds are open to a casual walk-through visit without charge.

History of the Maitland Art Center

The center's design and founding was the result of the vision of Jules André Smith (1880–1959). Smith was born in Hong Kong and grew up in New York State, where he attended school and graduated from Cornell University in 1902 with an undergraduate degree in architecture, and an MS degree in the same subject in 1904. He traveled in Europe and briefly practiced architecture before turning his skills to art, gaining wide reputation for his skills in sketching and drawing.

In 1917, he enlisted in the U.S. Army, serving in World War I as an officer. His background in art earned him an appointment to the Camouflage Corps. As both an officer and an artist, he commanded a small group of artists who documented the activities of the American Expeditionary Force in the war. On Smith's return to the United States after the war, he published a book of his wartime drawings, which received wide recognition. Titled *In France with the*

American Expeditionary Forces—Drawings by J. André Smith, the volume has been republished and is available online for a small fee.

In the 1920s, J. André Smith became involved in theatrical scene design and published a second book, which for many years was widely regarded as the authoritative text on that topic. In 1930, he and his studio assistant, Attilio J. Banca, traveled to Florida in search of a place to set up a studio and home, and stopped in Maitland. He met Broadway actress Annie Russell, who was teaching theater arts at Rollins College in neighboring Winter Park, and she introduced him to Mary Louise Curtis Bok, heiress of the Curtis Publishing Company family. Mary Louise Curtis had married Edward W. Bok, editor and publisher of the *Ladies' Home Journal*. As philanthropists and patrons of the arts, she and her husband financed

Decorative wall of art at the Maitland Art Center. Some have identified the Maitland Art Center as an example of Mayan Revival.

the building the Bok Tower, completed in 1929. It is now a major architectural attraction, located just north of Lake Wales, Florida, on the highest ground in the state.

Mary Louise Bok financed Smith's establishment of his art center in Maitland, which he designed. The construction was completed in 1937. With a total of twenty-two separate small buildings, including residences and studios, the Mayan-looking center, which he called the "Research Studio," was intended as an art colony. Smith continued to work at the Research Studio and, over his life, produced many prints and drawings. However, they were dispersed as gifts and he had no particular long-term dealer for his pieces, so there is no definitive, central collection of his work. The unique, Mayan Revival–style buildings, and the oddly named "Research Studio," now

Decorative doors at the Maitland Art Center. These doors, like many of the details at the art center, reflect a variety of cultural traditions.

operating as the Maitland Art Center, are lasting memorials to his unique vision. The cryptic "RS" over the entryway is a reference to his concept of a "research studio."

A stroll through the enclosed courtyard to the rear of the museum reveals a quiet and picturesque setting, with a lily pond and small, cubical whitewashed studio buildings, some decorated with Mayan-like and Christian-themed reliefs. The interior of the art center displays rotating exhibits, often including works by J. André Smith, such as the early

2020 show *The Exotic Realms of J. André Smith*. The center's guide to that show commented on Smith's varied talents, noting his "extensive body of work, including paintings, watercolors, sculptures, concrete reliefs, theater set designs, architectural drawings and architectural ornamentation."

Plan your visit: 231 West Packwood Avenue, Maitland, (407) 539-2181.

ORLANDO

The city of Orlando grew out of a small settlement and fort that was built during

Courtyard of the Maitland Art Center. The interior courtyard is surrounded by small artists' studios with a tranquil pond at one end.

the Second Seminole War, in 1838. Originally known as Jernigan, the community adopted the name of Orlando by 1856. Several legends surround the naming of the town, one suggesting it was adopted by a local judge who chose the name based on a character from Shakespeare's play *As You Like It*. The town remained a remote outpost until the 1870s, when it began to thrive as a center of the growing citrus farming in the region. Further growth came during the Florida land boom of the 1920s. The greatest boon to development came in 1965 and later, when Walt Disney chose to locate Walt

Disney World, which opened in 1971, nearby. By 2020, there were more than a dozen theme parks in the community, and the town has continued to expand, with a population estimated at nearly two million in 2020.

MUSEUMS

Mennello Museum of American Art

The Mennello Museum of American Art is in Loch Haven Cultural Park, which hosts a number of other facilities, including the Orlando Shakespeare Theater, the Orlando Science Center, the Orlando Repertory Theatre, Orlando Museum of Art, and the Orlando Fire Museum as well as periodic outdoor festivals. The park sits just to the west of Mills Street on the north side of Orlando, just about a mile south of the city limits of Winter Park.

The outside grounds of the Mennello Museum have developed into a major sculpture garden with works by Alice Aycock, Barbara Sorenson, Dale Rogers, and Paul Marco, among others. Several of the striking works by Alice Aycock that were installed in 2016 are on permanent exhibit. Two of them, *Twin Vortexes* and *Waltzing Matilda*, were first exhibited on Park Avenue in New York City. These two of seven sculptures, made of reinforced fiberglass, represent the energy flowing through the city of New York, based on the patterns of cyclonic wind patterns.

The small Mennello Museum maintains a permanent collection of American artist Earl Cunningham and rotating exhibits of other contemporary and past American artists. In fact, the main purpose of the Mennello Museum was to house and

The Mennello Museum of American Art.

Twin Vortexes. This sculpture by Alice Aycock is on the lakeside grounds of the Mennello Museum.

display the extensive collection of the work of Earl Cunningham. Cunningham was born in 1893 on a farm near Boothbay Harbor in Maine. Self-taught, he became one of the most prolific and well-known early twentieth-century American "primitive" (i.e., self-taught) artists. His images drew from his youth, when he lived in a fisherman's shack and worked on coastal schooners hauling freight along the coast from Maine to Florida.

L'homme by Robert Wolfe faces the lake behind the Mennello Museum.

Earl Cunningham visited Florida as a truck driver during World War I and spent winters in Florida with his wife in the early 1920s. He settled in St. Augustine in 1949, where he opened a small shop. His work was discovered there by the art collector Marilyn Mennello, who sponsored several exhibitions of his paintings, some at the Loch Haven Art Center, which is now the nearby Orlando Museum of Art. Cunningham died by suicide in 1977, but Marilyn Mennello preserved his works and they became the centerpiece of the Mennello Museum that opened in 1998.

Plan your visit: 900 East Princeton Street, Orlando, (407) 246-4278.

Orlando Museum of Art

This major museum, just to the north of the Mennello Museum, was founded as the Orlando Art Association in 1924, becoming the Loch Haven Art Center in 1960, with its present name adopted in 1986. Originally set up as an art center by a group of artists meeting informally to display and critique each other's work, the facility gradually expanded and then, supported by the community, moved into a large museum building designed by James Gamble Rogers III in 1960. At that point, "OMA" began collecting donated art and expanding with private and public funds. By 1969, the facility

Orlando Museum of Art.

had acquired a large auditorium, studio classrooms, a library, a storage vault, and offices, as well as extensive and well-lit gallery spaces, most of them named after primary donors of funds. By 2020 the museum had reached a total of eighty thousand square feet.

The collection includes more than twenty-four hundred individual pieces with concentrations in contemporary art, American art from the eighteenth century through World War II, and collections of ancient American and African art. A large and unique permanent collection is that of the Belgian postimpressionist painter Louis Dewis. Titled *An Artist's Life in France*, the collection occupies one gallery to itself.

University of Central Florida, Orlando

The University of Central Florida's School of Visual Arts and Design offers BA degree programs in art history, book arts, ceramics, drawing and printmaking, illustration, painting, sculpture, and type and design. It also offers BFA programs in emerging media, graphic design and experimental animation, and studio art. The programs are taught at the Visual Arts Building, 12400 Aquarius Agora Drive, at the university's main campus in Orlando.

Carl and Gini Weyand Gallery in the Orlando Museum of Art hosts changing exhibits.

The Church of Murelo by Louis Dewis is one of the works by Dewis, whose works were discovered after decades of obscurity. It is on display at the Orlando Museum of Art.

Louis Dewis (1872–1946) was born in Belgium and was inspired by French impressionists such as Corot, Monet, and Cézanne. He painted Belgian and French scenes of countrysides, villages, and cities. He was highly regarded in the 1920s and 1930s as one of Belgium's most distinguished landscape painters, and he was credited with reviving traditional landscape painting in contrast to the modern art trends of his own time. Dewis exhibited his works widely in the 1920s and 1930s in France and Belgium, as well as in Germany, Switzerland, and North Africa. During World War II, Dewis left Paris to live in Biarritz in the South of France on the Atlantic coast. During the war years, some of his works reflected the countryside of the Basque region of southwestern France.

On his death in 1946, his daughter, Andrée Ottoz, preserved more than four hundred pieces from Dewis's studio in Biarritz. After the work of Dewis had been virtually forgotten for five decades, the collection was "discovered" in the

1990s by Brad Fitz, an American-born great-grandson of Dewis. Fitz preserved the collection and arranged for its permanent display at the Orlando Museum of Art.

Among the other many rich displays at OMA are works by Edward Steichen, Stephen Althouse, Georgia O'Keeffe, and many individual pieces from the early American Hudson River school of landscape painters. The twenty-six-foot-long whimsical *Let Them Feel Pink* sculpture by Puerto Rican sculptor Carlos Betancourt has a small display space all its own.

Plan your visit: 2416 North Mills Avenue, Orlando, (407) 896-4231.

Let Them Feel Pink by Carlos Betancourt occupies a room all its own in the Orlando Museum of Art.

GALLERIES

There are three galleries operated by the Orlando city government. These "galleries" are more in the nature of museum exhibits—that is, the art is not for sale.

Terrace Gallery

The Terrace Gallery has movable walls in a twenty-four-hundred-square-foot area that can accommodate a wide variety of exhibitions.

Plan your visit: Orlando City Hall, 400 South Orange Avenue, Orlando, (497) 246-4279.

Mayor's Gallery

The "Mayor's Gallery" is a circular gallery on the third floor of city hall, dedicated to the works of central Florida artists. The rotating exhibits there each usually last about three months.

Plan your visit: Orlando City Hall, 400 South Orange Avenue, Orlando, (497) 246-4279.

Garden House Gallery: Harry P. Leu Gardens

This gallery in the Harry P. Leu Gardens presents revolving exhibits, including botanical themes, as well as works from the city's permanent collection.

Plan your visit: Harry P. Leu Gardens, 1920 North Forest Avenue, Orlando, (407) 347-7996.

There are about a dozen art galleries in Orlando, ranging from shops specializing in African art, to work by nationally recognized or local artists, to collective or collaborative shops. As noted elsewhere in this book, galleries, like other small retailers, open and close with changes in economic conditions. This listing shows a group of interesting galleries that were open early in the year 2020. Several are located in and near Colonial Drive in north Orlando, not far from the two museums mentioned above. However, there is no clear "gallery district" as found in some communities. Some of the smaller galleries have had exhibit space in the CityArts Factory, a local 501(c)(3) nonprofit organization, as noted below.

CityArts Factory

This is a nonprofit, large exhibit space, managed by the Downtown Arts District, hosting a variety of events, and several separate galleries. The galleries participating have included "Redefine Art," and "Zulu Exclusive," among others.

Plan your visit: 39 South Magnolia Avenue, Orlando, (407) 648-7060.

Bushman #1 Art

This African- and Afro-American-themed gallery hosts frequent events, including poetry readings and evening wine and painting sessions.

Plan your visit: 1023/1025 West Colonial Drive, Orlando, (407) 426-7355.

McRae Art Studios

This gallery and collective studio was formerly located in Winter Park, the suburban community just to the north of Orlando, and has a history as open to participation by local artists. It is one of the longest-established galleries in the area but only relocated back to Orlando in recent years. (See page 62 in Winter Park entry.)

Plan your visit: 1000 Arlington Street, Orlando, (407) 491-7712.

Grand Bohemian Gallery

This gallery is one of six operated by this unique luxury hotel corporation. The other locations include the Casa Monica in St. Augustine (originally built by Henry Flagler there); page 29, and four others, located in Mountain Brook, Alabama; Charleston, South Carolina; Asheville, North Carolina; and the "Mansion on Forsyth Park" in Savannah, Georgia. The organization was founded by Richard Kessler in 1984 and seeks to combine the bohemian tradition with luxury hotel accommodations in cities and locales known as cultural destinations.

Plan your visit: 325 South Orange Avenue, Orlando, (407) 581-4801.

Bronze Kingdom

This shop showcases a large private collection of bronze sculptures based on African masks and small African sculptures.

Plan your visit: 8249 Parkline Boulevard, Orlando, (407) 203-8864, or 3291 East Colonial Drive, Suite M-16, Orlando, (407) 203-8864.

Massimo Art Gallery

This gallery offers classes, entertainments, a wine and beer tasting bar, and frequent events.

Plan your visit: 11062 International Drive, Orlando, (407) 581-4801 or (407) 350-9218.

Snap!

This unusual local nonprofit organization operates two galleries devoted to photography and digital art. One is "Snap! Downtown," and the other is "Snap! Space," in the Mills 50 District. The director, curator, and cofounder is Patrick Kahn, and the organization's mission is "to celebrate master photographers and digital artists, discover and cultivate emerging talent, and promote the appreciation of photography and art worldwide"; the mission of the organization's events is to "boldly increase the visibility and appreciation of the photographic medium as a significant cultural art form, and broaden the demographic of engaged art enthusiasts and collectors within our community." A 2020 exhibit at the Snap! Space gallery on the gallery's tenth anniversary was an exhibit of works by Hollywood photographer Douglas Kirkland, whose iconic works included photographs of Judy Garland, Marilyn Monroe, Brigitte Bardot, and Mick Jagger.

Plan your visit: Snap! Downtown: 20 East Church Street, Orlando; or Snap! Space: 1014 East Colonial Drive, Orlando, (407) 286-2185.

Twelve21 Gallery

This gallery overlooks Lake Ivanhoe and stages themed monthly shows featuring local Orlando artists.

Plan your visit: 1221 North Orange Avenue, Orlando, (407) 982-4357.

MOUNT DORA

Mount Dora, in Lake County, is a small town with a population of less than fifteen thousand. The town is the home to an active theater group with a local community theater and also has several art galleries and other shops that benefit from a stream of visitors to the scenic location. The community's large annual arts festival and several smaller shows place the little village high on the list of Florida arts communities or arts destinations.

The town of Mount Dora had its origins in 1874 with early pioneering settlers. In 1880, the first postmaster for the community was Ross C. Tremain, who called the community "Royellou," a combination of the names of his three children, Roy, Ella, and Louis, now commemorated in a downtown alleyway. The nearby lake had been named Lake Dora after an early settler, Dora Ann Drawdy, and in 1883, the town was formally named Mount Dora. While hardly a "mount" in the eyes of many visitors from states like Maine or Colorado, the town does sit up from the lake on a plateau that is some 184 feet above sea level, and about one hundred feet above the level of the lake. For many years a local train took visitors on a scenic trip along the lakefront, but that line closed in 2017.

Sonya Watson, a local jewelry artist, told us that while the town may have had a reputation as an art colony in the 1970s, Mount Dora then became a mecca for antique shops for a few years. She told us that the increase in housing costs and the lack of inexpensive, affordable studio space have discouraged beginning or aspiring artists from settling in the town. Nevertheless, the presence of the annual arts festival and several flourishing galleries still make Mount Dora a destination for Floridians and out-of-state visitors interested in the arts.

MUSEUMS

Modernism Museum

This two-story museum first opened in 2013 and includes a large show space devoted to the studio arts movement. The studio arts movement is defined by the museum organizers as a form of modern art that combines craftsmanship, high art, and interior design. Many of the objects are functional furniture or household features

such as staircases. An associated shop across the street sells jewelry, clothing, gifts, toys, and a selection of art books related to the studio arts movement and to the museum itself. This museum is quite unique in Florida as it is owned by a local real estate enterprise, Main Street Leasing.

Plan your visit: 145 East Fourth Avenue, Mount Dora, (352) 385-0034.

GALLERIES

Artisans on Fifth

This is a not-for-profit, cooperative gallery, showing and promoting local and emerging artists.

Plan your visit: 134 East Fifth Avenue, Mount Dora, (352) 406-1000.

Modernism Museum Shop.

Blue Moon Studios/Sonya Watson Jewelry

Jewelry artist Sonya Watson operates Blue Moon Studios, renting space to other artists as well as displaying her own jewelry for sale. The gallery, along with the Jane Slivka Gallery, was previously located with the studio-shops of five other artists in a large office/commercial building one block to the east, but with the change of ownership there, all the smaller shops relocated. Ms. Watson explained to us that she hopes other artists and gallery owners will relocate to the 108 East Third Avenue locale, which has several available spaces along an enclosed courtyard. Among the artists who have shown work at Blue Moon Studios are Sharon Osterholt and Dodi Truenow.

Plan your visit: 108 East Third Avenue, Mount Dora, (352) 409-2442.

Jane Slivka Gallery

This gallery, immediately behind Blue Moon Studios, presents the work of one artist, Jane Slivka, who works with layered acrylic paints, many of them on oversized canvases. Jane Slivka also maintains her studio in the same space as the gallery. Jane had first visited Mount Dora in 2004 on a trip with a friend collecting antiques. Impressed with the charm of the town, she bought a house and stayed on. In her current shop, Ms. Slivka not only displays her own works, but also offers classes in design and composition in the studio space associated with the gallery. She earned a degree in art education from Ohio University, after studies in Boston and a semester abroad in Florence, Italy. She often spends summers traveling to North Carolina, Michigan, and Ohio and attends a number of art shows and festivals to display her work. She describes her own work as "a bit impressionistic," with many drawing inspiration from Florida coastal scenes.

Plan your visit: 108 East Third Avenue, Mount Dora, (352) 812-0546.

This scene by Dodi Truenow, a prolific artist in the plein air tradition, showing her works at the Blue Moon Studio.

Preserving Florida by Sharon Osterholt at Sonya Watson's Blue Moon Studios, Mount Dora.

Lauren Graham Cunningham

This small gallery shows the work of Lauren Graham Cunningham, who has been an artist in Mount Dora since 1999. She is active in the Mount Dora Center for the Arts and has won awards both in the United States and abroad for her paintings.

Plan your visit: 435 Dora Drawdy Way, Mount Dora, (352) 408-0703.

Painting Outside the Lines Art Gallery

This upstairs gallery shows the work of owner/artist Bev Neal and other eclectic artisans who work in a variety of media.

Plan your visit: 440 North Donnelly Street, #105, Mount Dora, (240) 731-1637.

Painting with a Twist

This studio is open for adults to attend in the evening, to take art lessons, and to bring their own bottle of wine. A bit offbeat, the studio is a franchise operation, located at the end of a busy shopping center outside the downtown area of Mount Dora on US Highway 441, and is one of reputedly five hundred franchises, including several others in Florida. The sessions cost between $25 and $45 per person. Originally the shops were known as "Corks and Canvas," which started in New Orleans after 2005's Hurricane Katrina.

Plan your visit: Tri-Cities Shopping Center, 16844 US 441, Mount Dora, (352) 383-7928.

Bev Neal

Painting Outside

THE LINES GALLERY

Featuring

- Original work by multiple artists
- Workshops
- Custom Designed Bicycle.Apparel

Renninger's Antique Center

Inside the city limits, but not in the village of Mount Dora itself, is this vast antique mall, one of the largest in the state of Florida. In the antique section of this mall (which also hosts a separate farmers' and flea market), about 180 dealers offer a wide variety of antiques, including furniture, decorative items, utensils, toys, and art, ranging from reproductions to valuable antique and collectible paintings. Renninger's also maintains operations in Melbourne as well as two other locations in Pennsylvania. Open Friday–Sunday weekly.

Plan your visit: 20651 US Highway 441, Mount Dora, (352) 383-8393.

EVENTS, TOURS, AND CELEBRATIONS

The small town holds tours as well as a large number of other annual events besides the major arts festival in February. Some of the festivals have been repeated every year for several decades.

Mount Dora Center for the Arts

Mount Dora Center for the Arts is a community center, offering fine arts gallery-style exhibitions, monthly "art strolls," an annual arts auction, and educational programs. The downstairs gallery space is open to aspiring artists. The many classes offered at the center include ceramics, drawing, mixed media, painting, photography, and printmaking. Staff in the upstairs offices of the center organize and promote the annual arts festival; as noted below, this large gathering of buyers and sellers is one

of Florida's largest and most successful outdoor arts festivals.

Plan your visit: 138 East Fifth Avenue, Mount Dora, (352) 383-0880.

Annual Arts Festival

Held annually in the first week of February (at the height of the "snowbird residence season"), in recent years this juried arts festival has hosted nearly three hundred exhibitors set up in canvas stalls in the main streets of the town, drawing a throng of more than two hundred thousand visitors. This event is one the largest arts festivals in Florida and certainly the largest for a town of this size. According to *Sunshine Artist* magazine's "200 Best" ranking of the best art shows across all of the United States, the Mount Dora 2016 show ranked number seven. In recent years, $20,000 has been distributed in prizes to exhibitors, with the Best of Show Award set at $5,000, two $1,500 awards, and some twenty $500 awards. The hundreds of artists report an average of $2,000 in sales; they remark that the crowds are not just there to view the art but include large numbers of serious buyers.

Plan your visit: 138 East Fifth Avenue, Mount Dora, (352) 383-0880.

Royellou Lane Tour

There is a monthly organized tour, in which visitors get a card punched at each outdoor exhibit and then enter the card in a raffle. The Royellou Alley or Lane tour begins at Fifth Avenue directly across from Donnelly Park and runs south for two blocks. The tour is held on the second Friday of every month (pending good weather). Among innovative features, the event allows participation by local high school students, who get to learn aspects of the arts business, such as showing their work and arranging sales, as noted by one of the early organizers of the tour, Sonya Watson.

Plan your visit: Mount Dora Center for the Arts, 138 East Fifth Avenue, Mount Dora, (352) 383-0880.

Florida Highwaymen Art Show

The annual Highwaymen exhibit is held in early August. This show, displayed at the Donnelly Building in Donnelly Park, 530 North Donnelly Street, is sponsored in part by the chamber of commerce. The exhibit provides an opportunity to view many of the works of this unique group of Florida artists whose works and careers are described more fully on pages 52–53.

Plan your visit: Heron Cay Resort, 495 West Old US Highway 441, Mount Dora, (352) 383-4050.

Mount Dora Crafts Show

On the third weekend of March each year, the town hosts a major crafts fair, with some 200 to 250 artisans showing their products. Quite a bit smaller than the art show, this event draws almost twenty thousand visitors, with products in a variety of categories. The crafts show, like the annual art show, is highly ranked by *Sunshine Artist* magazine on the national scale. Even so, many of the local craftspeople do not exhibit at the show, preferring to sell their work in established shops and galleries. The crafts show has been held annually since 1984, and like the larger art show, is held in canvas booths set up in the streets of the town.

Plan your visit: 411 North Donnelly Street, Mount Dora, (352) 217-8390.

ARCHITECTURE

Lakeside Inn

Still surviving from 1883 is Lakeside Inn, originally known as the Alexander House. The inn grounds include a small gallery and gift shop, the Gatehouse Gallery, which was built in 1908. The inn still rents rooms to guests and serves meals, including, in nice weather, service on the broad porch overlooking the lake. Below the inn, on the lakefront, excursion boats take visitors for a tour out on Lake Dora and a short ride along "Dora Canal," one of the many interlake canals that lead through thick Florida forests as well as residential areas.

Plan your visit: 100 Alexander Street, Mount Dora, (352) 383-4101.

Donnelly House

Among the architectural gems in town is the historic Donnelly House, now owned by the local Masonic Lodge, built in 1893 by the town's first mayor, John P. Donnelly. The striking yellow Queen Anne–style house, with bright zinc roofing and stained glass windows with Masonic emblems, is a local landmark, located at 535 North Donnelly Street.

LAKELAND

MUSEUMS

Polk Museum of Art

Among the more rural counties of central Florida, Polk County has a very active arts alliance, representing more than

The Gatehouse Gallery sells a wide variety of works by artists and artisans of Mount Dora and nearby communities.

These ceramic pieces by Amy Gentry are on sale at the Gatehouse Gallery at the Lakeside Inn, Mount Dora.

A masterpiece of Victorian architecture, the Donnelly House in Mount Dora is now a Masonic Lodge.

fifty nonprofit organizations, government agencies, and individual and corporate supporting members. The arts represented in this association include not only the visual arts, but also a variety of art fields such as theater, music, dance, poetry, film, and website design among others; the organization represents a variety of other cultural institutions such as historical societies. The alliance also maintains an artist registry designed to connect artists in a wide variety of fields with art lovers who seek to hire artists or commission works. For the visitor to Lakeland, the largest city in the county, the Polk Museum of Art and the nearby

group of Frank Lloyd Wright–designed buildings and structures at Florida Southern College are major art destinations.

This nationally accredited and Smithsonian-affiliated art museum is operated by Florida Southern College but is located a few blocks to the north of the college campus. Originally a private, community museum, the museum entered into affiliation with the college in 2017. The museum is free to the public, one of very few Florida art museums that do not charge admission. The museum building was designed by architect A. Ernest Straughn, a well-known Polk County architect. Straughn designed numerous schools and civic buildings in the area and other towns and cities in central Florida. He passed away in the year 2013. Straughn was an admirer of Frank Lloyd Wright, the internationally known architect. Wright designed twelve structures at Florida Southern College, and another there, the Usonian House, is based on a Wright design. The group of Frank Lloyd Wright structures is the largest collection of his work in the world. Guided and self-guided tours of the Frank Lloyd Wright structures are arranged through the Sharp Family Tourism and Education Center.

The Polk Museum of Art has an outdoor brick-enclosed courtyard, the Ann MacGregor Sculpture Garden, with works by James Bassham, Jane Jaskevich, Fonchen Lord, and Michael Mick. Visitors to the museum are sometimes surprised to find that much of the second floor of the building is devoted to a Montessori grammar school as well as to classes of the Florida Southern College Department of Art History and Museum Studies.

The museum, like most art museums, has a series of changing exhibits, but in the early 2020s, there are four multiyear exhibits. Two of them focus on photo-graphic depictions of human life all over the planet: *Material World* and *Hungry Planet*, both scheduled to continue until the year 2026. The first of these exhibits shows photographs taken by sixteen photographers of families in thirty coun-tries around the world, showing daily life, home, and possessions of the families; the second traces the travels of a couple, Peter Menzel and Faith D'Alusio, to briefly visit twenty-five families in twenty-one countries to observe what they ate. Both of these exhibits are intended to stimulate thought about "cultural commonalities and differences." A collection of their

Polk Museum of Art.

Introspection by Gino Miles.

photos documenting their travels formed the basis for their 2007 book, *What the World Eats.*

Another of the long-lasting "continuing" exhibits at the Polk Museum of Art is *Art of the Ancient Americas.* This exhibit presents artifacts collected in Mexico and Central America, and from the South American countries of Colombia and Peru. One collection focuses on *Warriors, Priests, and Rituals*, showing bound prisoners, warriors prepared for battle, and figures of priests. A second room presents artifacts on a country-by-country basis, as well as a display of archaeological methods. The emphasis in this second display is to show how the motifs and themes found in the artifacts of one culture may have been influenced by nearby cultures.

The fourth of the permanent or longer-duration exhibits is titled *The Von Wagner Code* and traces the puzzling problem of the picture *Claudius Triumph,* painted by Hungarian artist Alexander Von Wagner. Found in the collection in 2016 and restored, the display details the art-detective work in identifying the actual history of the painting, its artist, and the original's influence in modern culture, such as the modern notions of what chariot races were actually like. Reproductions of the painting were used in decorative playing cards in 1916 and in promoting the 1925 film *Ben Hur*. After extensive research, the picture was identified as an original by Alexander Von Wagner from 1882.

The painting had originally been identified as *Chariot Race* by Domenico Fetti, that had been given to the university and displayed briefly on campus before being taken down, rolled up, and stored. "Decoding" the problems associated with the painting engages visitors in the kind of mysteries that museum curators sometimes face when collection pieces have been misidentified or mislabeled, or in cases when the original documentation has been lost.

Among many thought-provoking and beautiful exhibits at the museum in early 2020 was an exhibit of artifacts from the private collection of Dr. Alan and Linda Rich. Before they had married, Dr. Rich had served in the East African Flying Doctor Service in Kenya, Tanzania, and Uganda. Unexpectedly, local craftsmen offered to trade art items for pieces of Rich's clothing. He realized the great opportunity to secure authentic, noncommercial pieces directly from the artisans. Later, traveling on medical care trips in Papua New Guinea and in West Africa, the couple expanded on the growing collection, gathering spiritual objects, such as masks and dolls, as well as relief carvings of village life. A small fraction of the Rich's extensive collection displayed

The Chariot Race by Alexander Von Wagner.

at the museum gave insight, not only into the cultures and religious practices of the places they visited, but also into their own humanitarian medical service among people with virtually no access to modern medicine.

Plan your visit: 800 East Palmetto Street, Lakeland, (863) 688-7743.

African Masks.

Mixed Media by Csaba Osvath on display at the Polk Museum.

MURALS

The small town of Lake Placid in Highlands County, another largely rural county in central Florida, has earned a reputation throughout the state as "the mural town," beginning with the painting of twenty murals in the period 1993–1997 throughout the town.

The idea of decorating some of the abandoned buildings, with their wide, dingy concrete walls, was the brainchild of Harriet and Bob Porter, who had traveled throughout the United States and Canada on a Gold Wing motorcycle, since retirement to Lake Placid.

Traveling through Vancouver Island in British Columbia, they discovered the little town of Chemainus, which had attracted tourists and revitalized its downtown by commissioning thirty-two murals depicting scenes from local history. The Porters immediately decided that the same principle would apply to Lake Placid, which at that time had at least fifteen empty stores and other buildings.

On their return to Lake Placid, they commissioned Thomas Freeman to paint a mural on the side of the Arts and Crafts Cooperative, which the Porters had cofounded along with the Lake Placid Mural Society. Completed in May

At the Masonic Lodge on North Main Avenue, this mural by Keith Goodson shows a selection of seven lakes of some twenty-seven that are close to the town of Lake Placid.

Tucked away at 148 East Interlake Boulevard, *Birding* by Thomas Brooks and Terry Smith is one of several murals in town dedicated to the local natural environment.

1993, the mural depicted a scene at Southwinds, the nearby resort founded by Melvil Dewey. Dewey, the inventor of the Dewey Decimal System used for indexing books in public libraries, had moved to the town in 1927, and it was he who pushed to change the name to Lake Placid, in emulation of Lake Placid, New York, where he had his northern home. Dewey had built a resort and arranged the renaming of the town, with plans to attract fellow New York State residents by echoing the New York name.

Since then, working with local financial sponsors, the society has arranged for the production of nearly 150 pieces of artwork in the town, including, by the year 2020, forty-nine large murals and about one hundred smaller items, including decorated trash cans and smaller paintings of birds and clowns.

From the beginning of the project, artists have depicted local historical characters and developments. In 1994, Roy Hampton and Terry Smith painted a mural of Melvil Dewey, standing holding a rolled-up plan of his intended improvements. Keith Goodson has continued his mural work and is responsible for at least eighteen of the larger murals.

All the murals in Lake Placid depict either aspects of the natural or human history of the region. For example, one large mural depicts all the various activities at a local county fair. Many of the murals have "hidden" features, such as very small animals, or incongruous elements, such as a pair of sunglasses in a historical mural.

Toby's Clown School grew out of a program started by Keith Stokes, a former Shriner's clown. With the establishment of Florida Hospital in Lake Placid in 1991, Stokes (as clown "Toby") visited the hospital, and soon calls for his cheerful visits came in from other regional hospitals. To meet the demand, Toby set up a "clown school" with six students at Florida Hospital, which soon expanded into a regular clown school, now a clown museum at Devane Park Circle, decorated with wall murals and a nearby trash container with a clown. Over the years the school graduated more than twenty-five hundred clowns, all dedicated to entertaining patients in hospitals, especially children. The clown theme shows up throughout the town in many smaller depictions of clowns in costume.

The effort to use murals to attract visitors and business to the town of Lake Placid has clearly succeeded, as numerous small businesses such as souvenir shops, barber shops, drugstores, and retail and service business of all kinds now thrive along Interlake Boulevard and Main Avenue, despite the fact that the town's population has steadied at the two

One of the largest and oldest of Lake Placid's murals, located at US Highway 27 and County Road 621 East, this mural captures the look of cattle drives that once headed from central Florida to the Gulf coast for shipment to Cuba. This was painted by Keith Goodson, who is responsible for more of the town's murals than any other artist.

On the corner of East Interlake Boulevard and North Main Avenue, this is one of the larger murals, showing activities at the Lake Placid County Fair. Painted by Connie T. Burns Watkins in 1996.

thousand to twenty-five hundred level in recent years.

Visitors to the town will want to pick up the catalog of murals, sold at local shops and at the Welcome Center/Mural Society/Chamber of Commerce building at the intersection of North Oak Avenue and Interlake Boulevard. The booklet tells the story of each mural and gives many details of the community's mural program.

All the murals reflect aspects of the local or regional history or environment in a literal fashion. For this reason, nearly every one of the murals in Lake Placid can be characterized as realistic and traditional in style, in contrast to the more abstract and contemporary art styles that dominate murals in other Florida communities such as St. Petersburg.

The local school for clowns is commemorated in dozens of clown images throughout the town of Lake Placid.

TAMPA

Some of the first landings of Spanish explorers in Florida were in Tampa Bay, but the region saw little settlement by Europeans or Americans until the United States acquired Florida in 1821. As the major port on Tampa Bay, the city of Tampa has developed into a center for shipping and naval operations since that period.

During the Civil War, the port was blockaded by the U.S. Navy; and later the city was occupied by Union forces, while Confederate blockade runners operated from the sheltered bay and nearby port towns like Bradenton. Tampa received a boost in national attention when Theodore Roosevelt assembled his force of Rough Riders there as part of the U.S. attack on Spanish-held Cuba during the Spanish-American War of 1898 that led to the independence of Cuba and the U.S. acquisition of Guantanamo and Puerto Rico.

Today, the large MacDill Air Force Base, situated at the southern tip of the city on the bay, is the headquarters for Central Command, which oversees U.S. armed forces in the Middle East. The city of Tampa has long been the economic anchor of the Tampa Bay area, with that military base supplemented by a commercial international airport; many light industries; a thriving financial and business center; and more than twenty colleges, universities, and other institutions of higher education.

An arts district located along the Hillsborough River just a few blocks to the north of the downtown business district houses a children's museum, an art museum, and a performing arts center. But like several other arts districts around the United States, this city-designated section does not host either art galleries or studio-residences of artists. Rather than suggesting a place where new art is generated, the "arts district" term here refers to the presence of nonprofit, publicly funded facilities that showcase the visual and the performing arts. However, the city parks department does operate a number of arts centers in various neighborhoods, which offer classes for children and adults in a wide variety of arts and crafts described below on pages 115–116.

MUSEUMS

Tampa Museum of Art

This civic arts museum, which recently celebrated its one hundredth anniversary, has specialized collections in these areas: Classical Antiquities, Prints and Photographs Related to Classical Antiquity, Decorative Arts and Sculpture, Modern and Contemporary Art, Works on Paper, 20th Century Photography, Modern & Contemporary Painting, and "New Media, Video, and Installation Art." This last collection, installed with a new building in the year 2010, consists of just a few works that include a light-emitting diode (LED) light installation, *Sky*, displayed outside on the south wall of the museum structure and a multimedia installation, *No Man City* by Jin Shan, which was commissioned by the museum to represent the museum's traveling exhibition *My Generation: Young Chinese Artists.*

Plan your visit: 120 West Gasparilla Plaza, Tampa, (813) 247-8130.

Scarfone/Hartley Gallery & R. K. Bailey Art Studios

The University of Tampa art faculty and local art patrons recognized in 1975 that the several temporary spaces on campus used for art exhibits were inadequate, so they got together to plan a dedicated exhibition space to accommodate both student and faculty works, as well as original works by recognized artists, and to hold art-related events such as guest lectures. Local architect Lee Scarfone agreed to design a space in a building that had been part of the original Florida State Fairgrounds, built in the 1930s as a New Deal Works Progress Administration (WPA) project. The frieze over the entrance to the present-day location of the university art gallery reflects the art moderne style characteristic of many New Deal–era public buildings.

Scarfone not only contributed his work but also provided a large part of the actual building cost. The Lee Scarfone Gallery, opened in 1977, was named in his honor. An additional grant by Mark Hartley, another local architect, resulted in the name "Scarfone/Hartley." The whole gallery was moved in the year 2004 to the Bailey Art Studios.

In the present, the gallery holds upwards of ten art exhibitions each year, changed periodically, displaying works by both students and professional artists, as well as holding a variety of community, music, and dance events. The gallery also hosts an artist-in-residence program in which the visiting artists work with students and create unique works. Visitors are encouraged to observe artists at work.

Plan your visit: University of Tampa, 310 North Boulevard, Tampa, (813) 253-6217.

Henry B. Plant Museum

Housed in a building that was originally the Henry B. Plant Hotel, built by the railroad tycoon as a lavish example of Moorish Revival architecture in 1889–1891, the museum contains exhibits from Henry Plant's own personal collections of antiques and art objects that he and his wife had assembled through extensive trips abroad, and that he had used in decorating the hotel. The museum collection also provides displays showing the Plant rail and shipping lines and documenting Plant's competition with Henry Flagler, who operated rail and shipping lines on the Atlantic coast of Florida. The hotel building and the museum collections of art, statuary, and other decorative artifacts and furniture echo the so-called Victorian or Gilded Age styles of flamboyant elegance. Among the collection are cloisonné vases, large and small statuary, cabinets and chairs with inlays of ivory or ebony, elaborate ceramic garden seats, and

The Henry B. Plant Museum on the campus of the University of Tampa, formerly the Plant Hotel, houses Victorian-era art and décor.

Japanese Imari ware—a type of highly decorative ceramic.

A few of the decorative art objects that the museum correctly identifies as examples of "conspicuous consumption" include a majolica floor vase with parrot and swan; a Louis XV–style borne, which was an elaborate circular couch; and a tête-à-tête, a form of Victorian love seat where the courting couple sat face-to-face, rather than side by side. As the museum's literature notes, these furnishings and art objects were testament not only to the era's lifestyle, but to the personal tastes of Henry Plant and his wife, Margaret.

Plan your visit: University of Tampa, 401 West Kennedy Boulevard, Tampa, (813) 254-1891.

University of South Florida, Tampa, School of Art and Art History

The University of South Florida in Tampa offers a BA in art history and a BA in studio art, as well as a BFA in studio art. The BFA program requires 82 out of the total 120 credit hours to be in art, while the BA requires 56 credit hours in art. As the college notes in its literature, the BFA program offers fewer opportunities to take courses outside of the major, a characteristic difference between BA and BFA programs in all colleges that offer both degree tracks.

Established in the early 1960s as a teaching museum, the USF Contemporary Art Museum has built a collection of more than five thousand objects. The USF Graphicstudio, established in 1968, has invited established artists, including both Robert Rauschenberg and James Rosenquist (see pages 156 and 117, respectively), to participate in the residency program, and the museum collection includes some of their works and others by well-known modern and contemporary artists, such as Roy Lichtenstein. Gifts from foundations have expanded the collection, including works from the Martin S. Ackerman Foundation in the mid-1980s, from Robert Stackhouse in 1991, and a gift from the Andy Warhol Foundation for the Visual Arts in 2008, consisting of more than one hundred original Polaroid photos and fifty gelatin-silver prints from the 1970s and 1980s. The museum's holdings also include a small teaching collection of pre-Colombian Meso-American artifacts. The public is welcome, but call for visiting hours.

Plan your visit: 3821 USF Holly Drive, Tampa, (813) 974-4133.

GALLERIES

Although the city of Tampa now has a population of over 385,000, it has far fewer art galleries than some much smaller towns in the state. This lack of galleries is probably because a large proportion of the city's population consists of students and young military or civilian families, rather than the more prosperous and older groups that make up some of the state's resort or retirement communities and beach towns. Without either a large population of art patrons or a steady flow of souvenir-seeking beachgoers, there is no ready customer base for a large number of galleries. However, there are four art galleries, one near the University of Tampa and three of them found in or near the Palma Ceia neighborhood, along MacDill Avenue.

Baisden Gallery

This two-thousand-square-foot gallery is located in a late nineteenth-century building directly across the street from the University of Tampa, with three separate exhibition rooms. A major focus of the gallery is contemporary studio glass or art glass, supplemented with photographs and paintings.

Plan your visit: 442 West Grand Central Avenue, Tampa, (813) 250-1511.

CASS Contemporary

Contemporary Art Space and Studio (CASS) has a focus on modern art from local, national, and international artists. The gallery presents exhibits, workshops, and lectures, as well as art-consulting services. The gallery counts among its customers not only private collectors, but also banks, businesses, hotels, and restaurants.

Plan your visit: 2722 South MacDill Avenue, Tampa, (813) 839-7135.

Michael Murphy Gallery

This gallery, which has been in business for more than twenty-five years, shows the work of a selection of sixteen or so accomplished artists in a sophisticated setting and offers a wide selection of frames, as well as delivery and installation services. The gallery maintains a relatively large Tampa staff in a five-thousand-square-foot gallery. Separate viewing rooms are provided for private showings.

Plan your visit: 2701 South MacDill Avenue, Tampa, (813) 902-1414.

Clayton Galleries

Clayton Galleries, opened in 1987 by Cathleen Clayton, has drawn many of its artists from the faculty at the University of South Florida Art Department, some of whom continued to sell their work through the gallery after they retired from teaching. Mark Feingold, who has assisted as manager of the gallery since 1994, developed an active framing business in the gallery, which has provided a steady "bread and butter" source of income for the gallery. Feingold holds degrees in fine arts and art education from the University of South Florida and had previously owned his own shops in Sarasota and in Provincetown, Massachusetts.

While showing us around the gallery, Feingold noted that Tampa, as a growing city with many new, working residents, has never matched the market for fine art of several much smaller Florida cities,

Sumerset by Jay Schuette, on display at Clayton Galleries, Tampa.

These pieces by William Bernstein are on display at Clayton Galleries.

such as Sarasota, which has been the home to twenty or more well-known artists as well as aspiring artists. Feingold anticipates that the Tampa market for fine art will gradually improve. In the years 2019–2020, Clayton Galleries featured many self-taught or "primitive" artists.

Although two other galleries noted above are found several blocks north of Clayton Galleries on MacDill Avenue, Feingold commented that the neighborhood was not really an "arts district" or "gallery district" as found in some cities. The designated "arts district" in downtown Tampa—the location of the art museum, a children's museum, and a theater for live musical and stage performances—has not become a mecca for galleries or artist studios, due to the high real estate rental and sales prices for downtown properties.

Plan your visit: 4105 South MacDill Avenue, Tampa, (613) 831-3753.

Gasparilla Festival of the Arts

The annual Gasparilla Festival of the Arts in Tampa, held annually since 1975, owes its name to a local legend that dates back to 1904. Every year since then, with one or two exceptions, Tampa organizations, called "krewes," in imitation of the Mardi Gras celebrants of New Orleans and Mobile, Alabama, have held a "Gasparilla" parade. Each of the krewes from Tampa and nearby communities develop elaborate floats, wear a variety of costumes (including many varieties of presumed outfits of pirates and their "wenches"), hold a parade watched by hundreds of thousands of celebrants, and reenact a

mythical landing by a pirate ship and its equally mythical captain, José Gaspar.

The arts festival simply borrowed the name from local tradition. The arts festival is a juried show, in that the three hundred artists participating are selected from about one thousand who submit applications. Food vendors and live entertainment, along with the arts on exhibit, draw crowds of 250,000 or more. Cash prizes are awarded, including a $15,000 Best of Show Award, and some $65,000 in other prizes in different categories. The financial firm of Raymond James, based in St. Petersburg, has provided financial support to the festival, recognized in the present-day official name of the event: "Raymond James Gasparilla Festival of the Arts."

Giclée

Mark Feingold explained the giclée print process for us. The term derives from the French giclée, *which means "to spray." This method of printing art uses an ink-jet method, similar in principle to computer printers. However, a giclée printer is far more precise and truer to the original colors of the pictured work, and the prints are therefore both more accurate and more expensive than previous art print technologies. Because of the cost of giclée print machines, many artists who seek this kind of print contact a service company rather than acquiring a machine for their own use. The companies offering the service can produce prints up to several feet in length and width, on canvas or fine-quality paper.*

Featured art at the festival includes ceramic and digital arts, drawing, fiber, glass, jewelry, mixed media, painting, photography, printmaking, sculpture, watercolor, and wood. In 2020, the first prize went to an elegant wood cabinet, *Hirukan V*, by Dennis Peterson of St. Marys, Ohio. In addition to the art displays, the festival also includes live entertainment, children's activities, and food vendors. The 2020 festival was held for the first time in the Julian B. Lane Waterfront Park, on the west bank of the Hillsborough River, directly across from the arts district, which includes the Glazer Children's Museum and the Tampa Museum of Art.

Harvey Park Sculptures

Through the early twentieth century, an active African American neighborhood thrived near the downtown area of Tampa. Although the neighborhood was later overtaken by "urban renewal," the once-active nightclub and entertainment district is now commemorated by Harvey Park, with a number of informative historical plaques and statues. At the entrance to the park on Cass Street, one of the most striking pieces of public art in Tampa is a colorful, larger-than life assemblage of sculptures by artist James Simon, representing the nightclub scene.

Plan your visit: 1000 East Harrison Street, Tampa, (813) 274-8615.

At the gateway to Tampa's Harvey Park, these sculptures by James Simon evoke the lively African American nightclub scene that thrived in the Central Avenue business district in the mid- and late twentieth century.

PUBLIC ART CENTERS AND PROGRAMS

The City of Tampa Parks and Recreation Department offers year-round art classes through programs at four studios located in different residential neighborhoods. Children and adults can work in pottery, clay sculpture, stained and fused glass, jewelry, silversmithing, drawing and painting, and other art media. In addition, the city operates an art center in a space at a major museum, and Hillsborough County operates another center in the Hyde Park neighborhood. The number of art centers in Tampa exceeds those found in any other city or town in Florida.

Taylor Art Studio

This studio focuses on pottery and glass fusing but also offers programs providing a wide range of creative after-school projects for children.

Plan your visit: 611 West Indiana Avenue, Tampa, (813) 274-8364.

Ybor Art Studio

Equipment at this studio includes eight potters' wheels and two electric kilns, a glass fusion kiln and equipment, and silk-screening utensils, as well as jewelry tools and equipment.

Plan your visit: 1800 Eighth Avenue, Tampa, (813) 242-5370.

Flowers by Makena.

North Hubert Art Studio

Classes offered include work in hand-built pottery, molded ceramic, woodworking, stained glass, and glass fusion.

Plan your visit: Westshore District, 309 North Hubert Avenue, Tampa, (813) 282-2911.

City of Tampa Golding Art Studio

This seventy-five-hundred-square-foot facility has nine indoor kilns, pottery wheels, a glass fusion work area, a jewelry studio, and a mixed media lab. The staff has more than forty-five years of combined education and work in the arts. They offer a range of classes including ceramic sculpture, oil painting, watercolor, small metal sculpture, jewelry, glass fusion, stained glass, fiber arts, printmaking, and other art forms.

Plan your visit: 522 North Howard Avenue, second floor, Tampa, (813) 259-1687.

In addition, the City of Tampa Visual Art Department has partnered with the Tampa Museum of Art to provide space for other programs. Classes have included printmaking, painting, drawing, and youth "portfolio building."

ST. PETERSBURG

St. Petersburg was founded by two late nineteenth-century developers. One was John C. Williams from Detroit, who had purchased land on Tampa Bay in 1876. The second was Peter Demens, who brought an early railway to the area in 1888. Demens had spent his youth in St. Petersburg, Russia, and according to legend, he won the coin toss with Williams as to which one would name the future settlement. Williams, the loser, named the first hotel in the new settlement after his home city—Detroit. Throughout the early twentieth century, the town grew into a major tourist and retirement community, attracting many winter snowbirds from the cold Northeast, traveling by rail, Greyhound bus, or auto, to enjoy the winter climate, the pelicans, and kitsch art, such as decorative items made from seashells—the art form known as "coquillage." The population of the city peaked at about 280,000 in the 1980s.

In the late twentieth century, the city of St. Petersburg, like many other urban centers across the United States, suffered from "urban flight"—that is, departure of many upper- and middle-class families to suburban and smaller towns, as well as the decline of some downtown business such as banks, hotels, groceries, department stores, and theaters that also moved out to suburban and outlying districts.

However, in recent years, a thriving art community has steadily contributed to rebuilding the life of the inner city. Spurred on by the philanthropy of several local families, St. Petersburg has become one of the most active and prolific arts communities in Florida, with four major art museums, more than twenty art galleries, four designated arts districts, programs of studio tours, and hundreds of large murals, some on major streets, with others facing alleyways or parking lots. In the years since 2015, the annual "Shine" invitational mural competition has added

James Rosenquist (1933–2017)

James Rosenquist grew up in Minneapolis, Minnesota, and at age twenty, he moved to New York City, where he studied at the Art Students League. He painted billboards for a living in Manhattan and Brooklyn in the period from 1957 to 1960, when he quit the billboard work after a friend died from a fall from scaffolding. He continued painting large works and soon gained fame for bringing the billboard style into exhibition art. As his works gained attention, he was credited as a leader of the pop art style, although he scoffed at attempts to group him with other artists such as Andy Warhol and Roy Lichtenstein.

His works, some of them the size of billboards or even whole rooms, continued to draw international attention and recognition. In 1971, Donald Saff, dean of the University of South Florida College of Fine Arts in Tampa, offered Rosenquist a residency in the college's Graphicstudio. Rosenquist moved to Florida and built a home and small studio in the remote, small coastal village of Aripeka, on the border of Pasco and Hernando Counties, about an hour's drive northwest from the university. Over the next decades, he accepted many commissions, working both from his own studio and from the USF facilities, including a thirty-seven-foot aluminum sculpture of a Band-Aid, which was installed in the year 2002 in the All Children's Pediatric Institute in St. Petersburg. At the university, he was known not only for his innovative and striking art, but also for his personal concern for fellow artists and former students.

Rosenquist continued to show his works around the world, receiving many commissions for public art. On April 25, 2009, a local brush fire swept through his property in Aripeka, destroying his home and two studios, as well as many stored paintings and works in progress. Rosenquist, however, continued to accept and complete numerous further commissions before his death in 2017.

many more murals to the downtown and outlying districts. Numerous facilities offering classes in specialties such as art glass and ceramics, as well as drawing and painting, contribute to making St. Petersburg a major center for the arts in the Tampa Bay region on the Gulf coast of Florida.

MUSEUMS

St. Petersburg Museum of Fine Arts
This major art museum was founded by Margaret Acheson Stuart (1896–1980) in 1965. Her goal was to establish an elegant and inviting place to show major examples of world art. By the year 2020, the museum had established a collection with more than twenty thousand paintings, sculptures, and artifacts including works by well-known artists like Monet, Georgia O'Keeffe, Willem de Kooning, and Auguste Rodin. In addition to European and American paintings, sculptures, and other art objects, the collection includes work from Asia, Africa, Mexico, and Central America, as well as Native American art. Informative panels place individual pictures in their artistic and historical context, explaining details such as the rise of the Barbizon school in France.

St. Petersburg Museum of Fine Arts.

The St. Petersburg Museum of Fine Arts includes two courtyard gardens, one serving as a sculpture garden, and both providing quiet spaces to rest. On the second floor, the Hazel Hough Wing brings in traveling exhibitions and private collections. Changing temporary exhibits bring visitors back to the museum over and over.

Plan your visit: 255 Beach Drive NE, St. Petersburg, (727) 896-2667.

Dali Museum

This museum is devoted to the work of one artist, Salvador Dali (1904–1989). The collection consists of more than twenty-four hundred pieces by Dali, including almost three hundred oil paintings and a variety of prints, sculptures, book illustrations, textiles, and varied objets d'art including whimsical furniture pieces. The building housing the museum is striking and unusual, with a geodesic glass bubble at the entrance, made up of more than one thousand glass triangular pieces.

The Dali collection was started by A. Reynolds and Eleanor Morse, who began their collecting after visiting a Dali exhibit at the Cleveland Museum of Art in 1942. Within a year they began collecting Dali pieces, and they met Dali in New York in 1943. By the 1970s, the Morse collection of Dali works overflowed their home, and they sought a permanent place to establish the collection as a separate museum. Reading of the Morses' search for a venue, a group of St. Petersburg civic leaders arranged for a museum devoted to Dali in 1982. The present building was completed and opened in 2011.

Dali was a unique artist throughout his long career. His early work reflected cubist art of the 1920s, but by the 1930s, his own surrealist themes and his flamboyant behavior attracted both critics and admirers. One of his early works that simultaneously fascinated admirers and enraged critics was *The Persistence of Memory*, completed in 1931. The painting showed soft, apparently melting pocket watches in a barren landscape, with some of the watches being eaten by ants, hinting at a message that time itself is fluid. Critics speculated whether he was seriously conveying a message, was playing a joke on the art world, or whether he was simply eccentric. With this and other works, Dali continued to baffle admirers and critics alike;

throughout the 1930s and 1940s and until his death in 1989, he remained a controversial and internationally known surrealist artist.

Plan your visit: One Dali Boulevard, St. Petersburg, (727) 823-3767.

James Museum of Western and Wildlife Art

This museum is based on the personal collection of Tom and Mary James and hosts more than four hundred works of art with a focus on the heritage of the American West. The Jameses' personal collection focused on several themes: the frontier, life in the wild, Native American artistic and tribal traditions, and wildlife art. The couple often purchased works of art in an effort to support emerging

Dali Museum exterior.

artists as well as to represent their favorite artistic themes. The galleries within the museum each have an individual focus: Early West, Native Life, Native Artists, Frontier, Wildlife, and New West. The Wildlife exhibits include photos of wildlife around the world, not just in the American West. Special collections include Native American jewelry and personal adornment.

Plan your visit: 150 Central Avenue, St. Petersburg, (727) 892-4200.

Morean Arts Center

The Morean Arts Center has its roots in the Art Club of St. Petersburg, established in 1917. The organization is devoted to art education and outreach to the community, with a range of classes; youth programs; exhibits; and several facilities for amateur, beginning, and established, advanced artists. The art center received an infusion of cash in 1996 with the donation of $1.6 million from Beth Ann Morean, the daughter of the founder of Jabil Circuits, a company manufacturing circuit boards for computers and other applications, that had grown from small beginnings in 1977 to a multimillion-dollar operation by the 1990s. In recognition of her generous gift, the new facility was named the Beth Ann Morean Center for the Arts (later shortened to the Morean Arts Center). The center does not charge admission, as a gallery with artwork for sale, with attached spaces with works in glass art, similar to the activities of arts centers in other communities. The organization has continued to foster arts education and to support the visual arts in a variety of media. In particular, the center's focus on glass art has made

St. Petersburg a major producer of this particular art form and the leading center for this art medium in Florida.

The Morean Arts Center hosts, in addition to its gallery space, a café, an art shop, and an information center for classes and programs offered. Several of the youth programs target children from disadvantaged or troubled homes. The Children's Learning Center is located in the building, which also hosts a "glass studio and hot shop" that contains a space for artists working in glass, as well as seating for observers. Glass art is available for sale at the gallery counter in the center.

The gallery space at the Morean hosts shows by individual artists, such as the early 2020 display of works by Perri Neri and Kirk Ke Wang. Discreetly, the individual pieces are labeled, but the prices for the works are not shown and are available on request. Past exhibits have included works by Jasper Johns, among others.

Plan your visit: 719 Central Avenue, St. Petersburg, (727) 822-7872.

Chihuly Collection

Across the street from the Morean Center is the Chihuly Collection, a ten-thousand-square-foot museum displaying the glass art of Dale Chihuly, established by the Morean Arts Center as a revenue-producing exhibit that helps support the other Morean Arts Center activities. The building itself was designed by award-winning, Cuban-born architect Alberto Alfonso, who now lives and works in the Ybor City neighborhood of Tampa. The structure is devoted to the works of

Chihuly Collection Building exterior.

Chihuly, whose works in glass and plastic appear in shows and permanent displays around the world. His striking *Florida Rose Crystal Tower* outside the museum is made from "polyvitro," a term he invented for one type of durable plastic suitable for outdoor sculpture. Chihuly began experimenting with this plastic for outdoor structures in the year 2000.

Plan your visit: 720 Central Avenue, St. Petersburg, (727) 827-4527.

Morean Center for Clay

Another facility of the same organization, the Morean Center for Clay, is currently located in the former Seaboard Line train station. This building, dating to 1926, includes studios for six well-established and forty-two aspiring ceramic artists. Equipment includes four kilns fired by wood and two fired by gas. Visitors can tour the facilities on Tuesday through Saturday. The facility also schedules

Columnar mural by Zulu outside Morean Center for Clay.

public tours and hands-on experiences for visitors.

Plan your visit: 420 Twenty-Second Street St. Petersburg, (727) 821-7162.

GALLERIES

The following galleries were in business in early 2020. However, due to the active and ever-changing art scene in St. Petersburg, others not listed here may be open or some of these may have expanded or moved to new locations. This listing represents a selection of some of the more than twenty art galleries in St. Petersburg (a city of less than three hundred thousand people), rivaling the number of galleries in Miami, which has a metropolitan area population of more than six million.

The Gallery

Established in 2013, this shop is open every day from 10:00 a.m. to 6:00 p.m., although such daily hours are quite rare in the gallery business. The focus of this gallery is on contemporary fine art, offering works in painting, photography, and sculpture by both local and internationally recognized artists. The shop offers consultation and installation services. The gallery space is also offered for private functions and meetings. Like other galleries, the Gallery participates in the "Second Saturday ArtWalk" until 9:00 p.m. The entrance is on the corner of First Avenue South and Second Street South.

Plan your visit: 200 Central Avenue, St. Petersburg, (727) 324-6730.

Florida CraftArt

This gallery is the headquarters of Florida CraftArt (FCA), a statewide, nonprofit organization of craft artists. Fine craft art is shown in this twenty-five-hundred-square-foot retail gallery as well as in the adjacent Exhibition Gallery that features curated exhibitions and programming. The Exhibition Gallery is organized more as an art museum than as a retail space. The second floor of the building has some nineteen or twenty artists' studios known as ArtLofts, as well as a meeting room (the "Creative Loft") that serves as a space for meetings, lectures, classes, and workshops. Like several other St. Petersburg galleries and studios, the studio spaces are open for visitors on the ArtWalk evenings, every second Saturday of the month from 5:00 p.m. to 9:00 p.m. (described further below). Visitors find the artists showing their works in the ArtLofts to be very friendly and willing to discuss their work.

Plan your visit: 501 Central Avenue, St. Petersburg, (727) 821-7391.

Luis Sottil Gallery

This gallery shows the work of Luis Sottil, a prolific artist born in Tampico, Mexico. His vibrant work, rich in colorful flowers, birds, fruit, fish, and insects, is a unique style that he named "naturalismo." His unique, vibrant style results from photo-graphing his subjects then working in paint to express their inner exuberance, using penetrating and unusual colors.

Plan your visit: 400 Beach Drive NE, Suite 150, St. Petersburg, (727) 220-1567.

Wyland Galleries

This gallery is owned by Wyland World-wide LLC, based in Irvine, California, which in Florida includes shops in Orlando, Key West, and Sarasota/St. Armands Circle. Like the other Wyland Galleries, this shop specializes in nautical-themed works and tends to present fine art, both wall art and decorative items, at the higher price range.

Plan your visit: 400 Beach Drive, Suite 146, St. Petersburg, (727) 201-8285.

Shapiro's Gallery of Fine American Crafts

This gallery specializes in "fine American crafts" and is a family-owned gallery dating back to 1998. The collection includes not only wall art but also a wide variety of crafts including blown glass, jewelry, metal sculpture, and works in clay. Sue Shapiro graduated in 1980 from the Massachusetts College of Art with a BFA in ceramics and began work in Amherst, Massachusetts. She moved to St. Petersburg in 1982 and began selling her work locally. Throughout the 1980s and early 1990s, her work began to receive national attention, and in 1998 she and her husband opened their first gallery in St. Petersburg; for nine years they operated a second store in northeast Georgia. The owners are very proud that their shop is a "multigenerational family business."

Plan your visit: 300 Beach Drive NE, St. Petersburg, (727) 894-2111.

Red Cloud Indian Arts

This gallery is devoted to the work of a group of artists, most of whom are Native American or Hispanic, and whose works reflect or build on Native American cultural traditions. The artists include Elvis Luna, Tony Weldon, Ira Lujan, Kevin Red Star, D YaeL Kelley, and Bob Canning.

Plan your visit: 214 Beach Drive NE, St. Petersburg, (727) 821-5824.

D Gallerie

This gallery shows work by both "emerging and accomplished artists from around the world." The gallery offers not only consultation regarding individual pieces, but also installation services where requested. Works include paintings, sculptures, original prints, and "wall climbers," by which they mean a unique sculptural form that appears to climb the wall on suspended lines. The gallery offers art at a very wide range of prices, and provides services to the serious collector of high-value art as well as the aspiring or beginning collector of more modest means.

Plan your visit: 153 Second Avenue N, B101, St. Petersburg, (407) 921-3608.

Ocean Blue Gallery

This gallery is associated with the one of the same name in Winter Park. This gallery features works with the sea and sea life as themes.

Plan your visit: 284 Beach Drive NE, St. Petersburg, (727) 502-2583.

Graphi-Ko

The owner is a specialist in jewelry art and in addition sells the work of other local artists.

Plan your visit: 669 Central Avenue, St. Petersburg, (727) 667-8126.

Sebastian Thomas Gallery

This gallery is owned by the artist David Frutko, a native of Baltimore who had worked for years in the advertising business in New York City. The gallery offers Frutko's own work, and he enjoys talking with customers about his current projects.

Plan your visit: 635 Central Avenue, St. Petersburg, (727) 258-4869.

Duncan McClellan Gallery

This large gallery specializes in glass art in the form of sculptures, vases, bowls, and decorative glass wall art, with hundreds of pieces on display. A sheltered outdoor space is comfortably furnished with couches to seat audiences for lectures and demonstrations, while a quiet rear sculpture garden displays a wide variety of three-dimensional pieces in different media. The ambience of the shop is enhanced by two mouse-vigilant, friendly cats.

Plan your visit: 2342 Emerson Avenue South, St. Petersburg, (855) 436-4527.

Woodfield Fine Art

Owned by artist Jim Woodfield, who maintains a small studio in the rear of the shop, this gallery offers the work of St. Petersburg artists, both those beginning their careers, and others with national or international reputations.

Plan your visit: 2253 Central Avenue, St. Petersburg, (727) 254-6981.

St. Pete ArtWorks

This gallery is another cooperative gallery, this one operated by the Gulf Coast Artists' Alliance (GCAA). The gallery has twenty-one participating members, each with designated wall space. The artists share the tasks of managing the gallery and keeping it open six days a week. During the Second Saturday ArtWalks, the gallery brings in local musical groups, and on the third Saturday of each month, the gallery presents a reception for the featured artist of the month.

Plan your visit: 2412 Central Avenue, St. Petersburg, (727) 710-7716.

Nuance Galleries

This gallery of long standing, operated by Rob Rowen, specializes in work by Cuban artists. In 2020, he shifted much of his operation to sales online; he can be contacted at nuancegalleries@earthlink.net.

Plan your visit: 2924 Central Avenue, St. Petersburg, (813) 875-0511.

ARTS DISTRICTS

There are five established arts districts in St. Petersburg, each characterized by the locales of several art galleries and studio groups. The five established districts are:

Waterfront Arts District

This district includes both the Dali Museum on the south and the Museum of

Fine Arts on the north, and running from Beach Drive west to about Third Street.

Central Arts District

From Third Street on the east to about Martin Luther King Street on the west, and from First Avenue South to First Avenue North. This district includes the Morean Arts Center, the Chihuly Collection, and several of the galleries listed above.

The Edge

Just to the west of the Central Arts District. This district is just getting its beginnings in the 2020s.

Warehouse Arts District

This district includes two major arts studio complexes, as well as several galleries. West of Interstate 275 and south of Central Avenue, St. Petersburg.

Grand Central Arts District

Started in the year 2020, the Grand Central Arts District is to the north of the Warehouse Arts District. This arts district has not yet developed a large art presence. However, given the search for inexpensive studio space and the constantly growing art community in St. Petersburg, it is expected to emerge as another thriving arts neighborhood.

STUDIO TOURS

Various studios are open to visitors at least once a month. Among the studios offering such "open house" afternoons and/or evenings are these two:

Arts Exchange/Gallery

Second Saturday ArtWalk, 5:00 p.m. to 9:00 p.m.

Plan your visit: 515 Twenty-Second Street South, St. Petersburg, (727) 256-0821.

Five Deuces Galleria

First Saturday and Sunday 10:00 a.m. to 4:00 p.m.; and the Second Saturday ArtWalk, 5:00 p.m. to 9:00 p.m.

Plan your visit: 222 Twenty-Second Street South, St. Petersburg, (727) 906-1223.

Several of the other studio facilities offer once-a-week or more frequent open houses or tours. One established and convenient tour is the organized Second Saturday ArtWalk, which covers more than forty galleries as well as the studio groups noted above. The organizers point out that it is impossible to visit *all* the galleries and studios on one tour. The bus trolley conveniently stops and drops off visitors and returns in a cycle to pick up passengers to proceed around the loop, which includes all five districts. Free street parking is available for tour participants.

Plan your Second Saturday ArtWalk visit: (727) 518-5142.

MURALS

Visitors to St. Petersburg are surprised to find the downtown and outlying districts decorated with hundreds of murals, found on the exterior walls of both active and abandoned buildings, facing parking lots and alleyways as well as major streets. The art of the murals varies from extremely detailed "fantasy art," portraiture, abstract forms, and works

Emma Rubens mural, downtown St. Petersburg.

reflecting pop art of various kinds ranging from cartoon art to graffiti, to works echoing the styles of the great Mexican muralists of the 1930s or evoking themes of Florida history.

Since 2015, an invitational mural contest, "Shine," sponsored by the St. Petersburg Arts Alliance, has added more than 120 murals to the growing collection.

Zulu mural: *Girl with Music*, downtown St. Petersburg.

Mikael mural, downtown St. Petersburg.

Taloc by Daniel Barojas, downtown St. Petersburg.

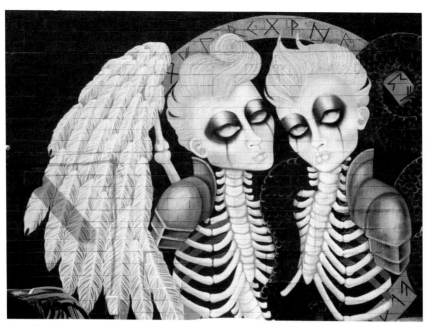

Two Skeletons mural, downtown St. Petersburg.

While guides to the Shine collection are available online, the vast production of murals appears to outpace any attempt to definitively catalog the works. It is common to see individuals or groups of tourists and locals photographing murals with equipment ranging from professional cameras to iPhones. Among the many prolific mural artists are "Zulu Painter" (Carlos Culbertson), Bekky Beukes, Emma Rubens, Sebastian Coolidge, and Derek Donnelly (who organized a mural-painting collective known as "Saint Paint Arts.")

SAFETY HARBOR

Like other several other small towns in Florida that have developed reputations as centers for the arts, Safety Harbor has a unique history. It was at this point on the west coast of Florida that one of the first Spanish missionaries to the territory was murdered by the local natives when he attempted to land in peace. Father Luis de Cancer, his landing, and his martyrdom are commemorated in a small church close to his actual landing point in this shallow reach of Tampa Bay.

Father Luis de Cancer de Barbastro was an advocate of peaceful conversion of the Native Americans, rather than conversion by conquest, and he had worked among the natives of Guatemala with some success. In 1549 he led a group of missionaries to Tampa Bay aboard a caravel, a very small sailing ship. Despite being warned by the ship captain of the danger of landing, on June 26, 1549, de Cancer rowed toward shore with two other friars.

Stained Glass Window in the Espiritu Santo Church. Artist unknown.

Watching from the boat, his companions were stunned to see the native Tocobaga group ashore beat de Cancer to death with heavy sticks. The spot of the tragedy is in or near the present-day Philippe Park along the shore of Safety Harbor. After the episode, the Spanish made no formal effort to make contact with the local Tocobaga people for twenty years, and then only cautiously.

Plan your visit: 2405 Philippe Parkway, Safety Harbor, (727) 726-8477.

The Philippe Park and the parkway itself are named for another colorful character in the story of Safety Harbor, Odet Philippe, who established a plantation on the grounds of what is now Philippe Park. Philippe was born in Lyon, France, in 1787, and moved to Pinellas County in Florida, taking up a land grant in Safety

Harbor in 1843. An inveterate storyteller and enterprising businessman, he experimented with planting grapefruit and ran a small cigar factory, a bowling alley, and an oyster bar, with some of the enterprises in what is now downtown Tampa. Some of his claims about his past were clearly tall tales to impress his customers and friends—for example, he claimed to be of noble birth, and to have been a classmate of Napoleon (given that he was born when Napoleon was aged eighteen, that seems highly improbable). In fact, researchers have concluded that he came from a more humble background, having spent his youth on the island of Saint-Domingue—now Haiti.

The large waterfront resort Safety Harbor Resort and Spa, at the intersection of Bayshore Drive and Main Street, whose origins date back to the 1920s, is on the site of a set of springs, and was originally a "spa" in the European sense, where visitors came to drink the spring water. In the late twentieth and early twenty-first centuries, the town of Safety Harbor developed a reputation as an art colony, with frequent arts and crafts yard sales and street shows. Safety Harbor Resort and Spa continues to draw many visitors who stroll along Main Street and nearby blocks to explore the several art galleries and the murals that now decorate some of the building façades.

MUSEUMS

Safety Harbor Museum and Cultural Center

Among the local history collections owned by this museum is a selection of Highwaymen paintings, which, depending on the changing displays and limited space in the museum, may or may not be available for viewing.

Plan your visit: 329 Bayshore Boulevard South, Safety Harbor, (727) 724-1562.

GALLERIES

Syd Entel Galleries/Susan Benjamin Glass, Etc.

These two shops, with an associated frame shop, are among the first to encounter in a walk along Main Street from the waterfront. The two shops present fine art, in paintings and quality glass art, with one-person artist shows that are changed frequently.

Plan your visit: 247 Main Street, Safety Harbor, (727) 725-1808.

Harborside Studios

This shop carries many small and highly colorful works of wall art, as well a selection of jewelry.

Plan your visit: 176 Fifth Avenue North, Safety Harbor, (727) 601-1884.

Safety Harbor Galleria

This nearby shop has a colorful exterior and sells a wide variety of local art and clothing.

Plan your visit: 123 Second Avenue South, Safety Harbor, (727) 700-1600.

Safety Harbor Art and Music Center

This building is highly decorated, and features a fanciful, decorated elephant in front, on the corner of Second Street North and Seventh Avenue. An open-air stage faces a courtyard, and frequent concerts, performances, and events make this the art and music cultural center of the community. After the building was completed, local artists and craftspeople got together to cover the building with shiny chips in many mosaics, reflecting the bright and full-coverage, decorative art style that characterizes the "Whimzey-Land/Bowling Ball House" nearby.

Plan your visit: 702 Second Street North, Safety Harbor, (727) 725-4018.

WhimzeyLand/Bowling Ball House

The owners of the "Bowling Ball House" also painted the mural *Whimzee the Manatee* at 605 Second Street North. The Ramquists, with their lighthearted approach to exterior décor, have spread their ideas to several other nearby properties and with their own mural work.

Bowling Ball House.

The couple are often on tour to other communities with their art, but when home, they hospitably explain their work and host visitors around their yard, which is a work of art in itself.

According to the story they tell visitors, the idea for using bowling balls as décor developed when Todd Ramquist ran across a closed bowling alley that offered ten bowling balls free to anyone willing to take them away. He enlisted Kiara to take her share, and then others, accumulating a total of about sixty, which they proceeded to use in decorating their house and yard. A tree with glass bottles and numerous other colorful artifacts and mosaics have made their home one of the more famous art sites in the state of Florida, regarded by some as "kitsch" and by others as experimental fine art.

Plan your visit: 1206 Third Street North, Safety Harbor, (727) 725-4018.

Owl by Jen Pearl.

MURALS

Murals scattered throughout the town reflect a variety of styles, with some similar to the Ramquists' work, and others ranging from fantasy art to local historical scenes, to vibrant visions of undersea life. On the west side of 885 Second Street North, facing the railroad track, is a row of murals that can be viewed as a group from across the railroad track facing Ninth Avenue North.

Other murals are found through the town, with one on the corner of Main and Harborside Boulevard, facing Harborside Boulevard, honoring Odet Philippe. This historical mural depicts Philippe with the grapefruit that he introduced to Florida.

Elephant by Beth Warmath.

Manatee mural by Mason Schwake.

Blue Fish and Turtle mural by Yhali.

Manatee mural at the Pancake House.

BRADENTON

Bradenton, situated on the Manatee River a few miles to the south of the Tampa Bay area, is in the midst of an area with many historical associations. The original landing place of the Spanish explorer Hernando de Soto, in the year 1539, was at some point nearby on the Manatee River, now commemorated in a small park and historic site a few miles west of downtown Bradenton, at Shaw's Point, off Seventy-Fifth Street NW.

Just across the river from Bradenton, in the small town of Ellenton, is the historic Gamble Plantation home. This building has a unique history, as it was a stop on the adventurous escape of the Confederate States' secretary of state, Judah Benjamin, who fled capture by Union forces on his way to sanctuary in

Great Britain at the end of the Civil War. Because Benjamin was a leader of the Confederate secret operations, the U.S. government offered a reward of $50,000 for his capture as a suspect in connection with the assassination of Abraham Lincoln. The award amount was extraordinary for the era—the equivalent of more than $788,000 in 2020. Benjamin eluded capture and fled by sea to Britain by way of the Bahamas; he never returned to the United States.

Another historical site of interest in Bradenton itself is Manatee Village, at 1404 Manatee Avenue East. The attraction is an assembled replica village of homes, a store, school, church, and other buildings that replicate the lifestyle of nineteenth- and early twentieth-century "cracker" families of central Florida.

De Soto Trail Monument.

Arte Coyacano Gallery in the VOTA district of Bradenton.

Bradenton also hosts an excellent museum detailing the history of Florida: the Bishop Museum of Science and Nature at 201 Tenth Street. Despite the museum's name with its emphasis on science, its collection does an excellent job of covering the history of Florida's Gulf coast, with exhibits detailing many aspects of Florida history from prehistoric periods to the present. Ample parking for this museum is available near the Tenth Street entrance.

Today, the town of Bradenton is engaged in a serious and successful effort to establish a "Village of the Arts" in the tradition of working art colonies, in a neighborhood just to the south of the downtown section, where the art center is located.

Art Junkies.

One of the longest-established galleries in the Village of the Arts is that of French-born artist Joan Peters at 1210 Eleventh Avenue West. Joan's work includes abstract pieces, but she notes that many buyers expect to shop for landscapes and seascapes featuring uniquely Florida scenes—they are looking for palm trees, she says, and they want a memento of their stay in Florida, so she includes many such scenes in her repertoire. Some of her work, she told us, is almost like folk art in its simple, direct style.

Joan Peters was born in Paris and had always wanted to study art, having often visited the Louvre and the Musée du Jeu de Paume. However, her father insisted she do something more practical. She

told us that he said, "We don't need a starving artist . . . we need a lawyer." She remembers, in those days, you did what your father said, so she graduated with a law degree.

However, she also attended the Ecole du Louvre, studying design and art history. She moved to the United States in the 1970s; she later moved to Sarasota in the year 2000 and then in 2001 settled in the Village of the Arts in Bradenton.

She has pursued her love of art with a variety of media, including book covers as well as book illustrations, paintings, and posters. She explained to us that she enjoys work in the plein air tradition, working outdoors and painting from nature along with a group of other artists. Although she has substituted

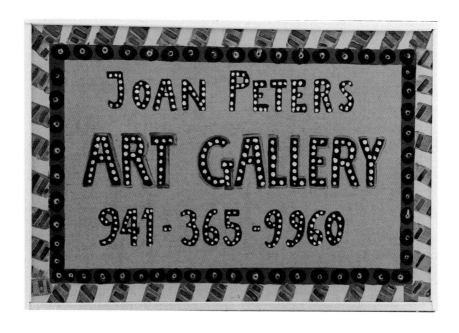

Inside Joan Peters Gallery.

as a teacher at ArtCenter Manatee, she said that she prefers "to do what I want to do, and what I want to do is paint." Among the many unique items in her gallery-shop are depictions of skeletons from the Day of the Dead celebrations on the first Friday of November every year, echoing the Mexican cultural tradition.

Plan your visit: 1210 Eleventh Avenue West, Bradenton, (941) 365-9960.

Joan Peters Gallery.

ART CENTERS AND TOURS

ArtCenter Manatee

Located in the business section of downtown Bradenton, directly across the street from the rear side of the Bishop Museum of Science and Nature, is ArtCenter Manatee on the corner of Ninth Street and Third Avenue West. There is parking to the rear of the building off Third Avenue West. The center has a long history, established in 1937, and its ten-thousand-square-foot building contains three art galleries, five classrooms, a gift shop, and an art library with more than three thousand volumes. Parking spills over onto the grass; when we asked if a meeting was in progress, a staff member told us no, the crowd was just due to the usual attendance at classes.

The center holds a wide and impressive variety of arts and craft classes in its classrooms. The catalog of classes at the art center details courses that run for various periods, some once a week for five or six weeks, with separate sessions throughout the year. The courses are open to various levels of experience and focus on such specialties as acrylic painting, portrait painting, mixed media, figure drawing, pen and ink, and work in both oil and watercolor. Other courses and workshops focus on photography, silk painting, silk scarf painting, marbling, pottery sculpture, jewelry, and glass art, for a total of more than one hundred separate classes and workshops, most with multiple schedules through the year.

Exterior of ArtCenter Manatee.

The center also arranges open and member-only juried shows for artwork completed in the last three years, with sculpture exhibits open to works completed in the last five years. Exhibits in the galleries are changed every month and display not only local work, but also art by regional and national artists. Monthly receptions are held in the evening, open to the public at no charge, where exhibiting artists are available to discuss their works.

Membership in ArtCenter Manatee includes a variety of benefits, such as access to the center's library and to the open studio, as well as discounts on purchases and on events such as shows and lectures.

Plan your visit: ArtCenter Manatee, 209 Ninth Street, Bradenton, (941) 746-2862.

Sculpture at Mary and the Dude Gallery.

Other gallery/homes featuring the work of local artists in the Village of the Arts (VOTA) open in 2020 totaled at least twenty-five. However, because of the influx of new artists, closures and occasional relocation within the village, and other changes, visitors may care to pick up from one of the galleries or download from the internet a local current list or map. The hours of opening vary, but most are open Thursdays–Saturdays, from eleven in the morning until four or five in the afternoon. Since most of the galleries are operated by the resident artist, without assistants or managers, business hours necessarily vary considerably due to personal errands, illness, working on a project, or other obligations.

VOTA does not maintain an official office or headquarters, but a self-guided walking tour can be planned with a map downloaded from https://www.villageof thearts.com/map/. A convenient way to view a group of gallery-studios is to park your vehicle and stroll along, spotting any that happen to be open.

Plan your visit: Between Ninth Street West and Fourteenth Street West, Bradenton.

Village of the Arts banners like this are found throughout the neighborhood.

SARASOTA

Sarasota has a wide variety of institutions directly supporting the arts, including museums, an art college, a very successful art center that offers classes and juried shows, and a few art galleries, as well as several small neighborhoods with reputations as art colonies. A major attraction in all this artistic activity and interest is the estate of John Ringling, the circus owner who built a magnificent mansion in Sarasota in the 1920s.

MUSEUMS

Ringling Museum of Art

The museum as well as the other attractions on the estate are open for touring, with a variety of ticket package rates. Tickets may be purchased online, or at the property.

The Ringling Museum of Art's collection includes over twenty-eight thousand works, which began with Ringling's original interest in the "Old Masters." This term is used to refer to European painters or sculptors from the Renaissance period (early 1400s through the 1700s). Generally, these painters studied under another artist, in a relationship similar to the "apprentice-master" relationship in many crafts and trades. While present-day art critics tend to avoid the term since its definition is a bit broad, it is still used by many museums to refer to accomplished European painters or sculptors who worked during that four-hundred-year time period, or to one of their works, with individual works identified as an Old Master.

The Ringling collection has expanded well beyond that original Old Master focus, and now includes both Western and non-Western art from ancient times through the nineteenth century, as well as American artworks from the early 1900s to the present. The library not only contains works bearing on the art collection, but on the history of the circus, and on John Ringling himself. In addition, the museum hosts a website that describes not only the art, but historical documents and photographs in the Ringling collection. Information on nearly forty-five thousand of the items in the mansion, the circus museum, and in the museum of art can be viewed online at https://www .ringling.org/, along with images of many of the pieces.

Plan your visit: 5401 Bay Shore Road, Sarasota, (941) 359-5700.

Sarasota Art Museum

This large art museum, which opened in late 2019, is listed in its literature as a "*kunsthalle*," that is, an art museum with no permanent collection of its own but relying on showing art on loan from individuals or from other institutions. The German word, meaning "art hall" or "art shed," is used to distinguish such institutions from a *kunstmuseum*. There is no exact equivalent word in English for a museum relying on loaned art, so the Sarasota Art Museum employs the German term.

The museum's initial displays in 2020 included not only a composite, polyure-

Sarasota Art Museum.

thane, plexiglass, and aluminum full-scale Ferrari Berlinetta car—*Mnemonic Vehicle No. 1*, by Vik Muniz, displayed on the first floor—but also a larger exhibit of works by Muniz on an upper floor of the museum. The Muniz works include many focused on the garbage collectors of Rio de Janeiro, Brazil, the *catadores*. Working with Muniz, the workers helped to arrange large portraits of themselves

Mnemonic Vehicle No. 1 (Ferrari Berlinetta) by Victor Muniz.

using items from the trash on the floor of a large warehouse. Muniz would photograph the portraits, which from a distance, become works of art. The proceeds from the *Pictures of Garbage* prints were donated to a cooperative the workers had set up to improve life in their community.

The Muniz exhibit also includes works he did to create fresh originals based on the works of some of history's greatest painters, including, among others, Caravaggio and Andy Warhol.

Plan your visit: 1001 South Tamiami Trail, Sarasota, (941) 309-7662.

GALLERIES

Madeby Gallery, Ringling College of Art and Design

A few blocks to the south on Tamiami Trail is the Ringling College of Art and Design, with its Madeby (pronounced "made by") Gallery. This small shop and gallery shows the work of students

Madeby Gallery. Ringling College of Art and Design.

and alumni (and some faculty who are themselves graduates of the college). The works include art, photos, greeting cards, sculpture, and even furniture and toys,

Madeby Gallery displaying works by students and graduates of Ringling College of Art and Design.

among other items. Between the gallery and Tamiami Trail is a small gravel-covered sculpture garden displaying several works by former students.

The Ringling College of Art and Design has seven other galleries and halls that display the work of faculty and students, all of which can be located on a map provided at the Madeby Gallery: the Patricia Thompson Gallery, the Alyce and Edward Kalin Gallery, the Lois and David Strulberg Gallery, the William G. and Marie Selby Foundation Gallery, the Crossley Gallery, the Richard and Barbara Beach Gallery, and the Willis A. Smith Construction Inc. Galleries. For hours and details of exhibitions, consult www .ringling.edu/galleries.

Plan your visit: 2700 North Tamiami Trail, Sarasota, (941) 822-0442.

Ringling College of Art and Design, Sarasota

Unlike the other colleges and universities listed here, the Ringling College of Art and Design offers majors only in art-related fields. Its courses and degrees are accredited and fully recognized as college level by university and college associations. The college offers a BA program in the business of art and design and BFA degrees in twelve art specialty majors: computer animation, creative writing, entertainment design, film, fine arts, game art, graphic design, illustration, motion design, photography and imaging, virtual reality development, and visual studies. Ringling also offers a graduate program in conjunction with Florida State University in Tallahassee. The college maintains a number of museum-style galleries on the campus.

Madeby Gallery sculpture.

Along South Palm Street in the center of downtown, there used to be an extensive "gallery row" with more than a dozen art galleries. Today, as David Dabbert of Dabbert Gallery pointed out to us, the number of galleries has shrunk, with just three—his own, the nearby Galleria Silecchia, and Palm Avenue Art—still in business. Dabbert attributed the decline to uncertainty about the financial future in the years 2018–2020.

Dabbert Gallery
This gallery maintains a focus on artists with national or international reputations.

Plan your visit: 46 South Palm Avenue, Sarasota, (941) 955-1315.

Galleria Silecchia
This gallery offers works by contemporary paints, sculptors, glass artists, and ceramicists. In addition, the shop sells some limited edition bronze sculptures.

Plan your visit: 20 South Palm Avenue, Sarasota, (941) 365-7414.

Palm Avenue Art
This gallery shows the works of more than sixty artists, many with international reputations. The offerings include numerous seascapes and nautical scenes, among a wide variety of other works of the highest quality.

Plan your visit: 10 South Palm Avenue, Sarasota, (941) 388-7526.

Art Uptown Gallery
Art Uptown showcases thirty artists from the west coast of Florida, including quite a wide variety of media, including glass and ceramic sculpture as well as painting. The gracious staff are happy to show visitors the items on offer.

Plan your visit: 1367 Main Street, Sarasota, (941) 955-5409.

Art Uptown Gallery interior.

Curated and Juried Shows

Some art centers and many museums conduct either curated or juried art exhibitions. These two types of art exhibitions are similar in that they bring art from a variety of artists, reflecting a chosen theme, for a temporary exhibit in the facility. But the two types of exhibits are quite different in other ways. In a curated exhibition, a single curator chooses the focus and theme of the exhibit, chooses its title, and also selects the individual works by invitation. The curator not only defines the theme, but also searches out individual pieces of artwork that reflect the curator's own concept of the theme. Further, the curator usually has a say in developing the installation of the work and in preparing the catalog. In effect, a curated exhibition is a product of the curator's conception and work.

By contrast, a juried exhibition begins with a competitive call for entries, *usually to reflect a theme. However, not all works submitted will conform to the theme, and the jurors usually do not know the identity or reputation of the artists submitting entries. While the jurors decide which works submitted will be included in the exhibition, thus making it competitive, jurors or judges rarely have any say in how the work is displayed, how it is labeled, or in preparing the catalog of the exhibition, details usually arranged by the museum or art center.*

A few blocks farther south, at the busy intersection of Tamiami Trail and Route 789—the John Ringling Causeway that leads out to St. Armands Circle—is a massive outdoor statue titled *Unconditional Surrender*. This work by Seward Johnson (who also sculpted the dancing couple in front of the Key West Museum of Art

Unconditional Surrender by Seward Johnson.

and History and other outdoor statues in Key West) commemorates August 14, 1945, when the "greatest generation" celebrated their victory in World War II. The sculpture models an iconic photograph of a sailor kissing a nurse in Times Square after crowds gathered when hearing of "V-J Day," the surrender of Japan. The title of the statue evokes not only the "unconditional surrender" of the Japanese Empire at the end of the war, but has a double entendre in the pose of the nurse in the sailor's embrace.

A veteran of World War II, Jack Curran, purchased the statue and donated it to the city of Sarasota. The statue has been in the news over the years, both because some thought it inappropriate and because *Life* magazine sued Johnson, the sculptor, for infringement of copyright of the photograph by Alfred Eisenstaedt, who snapped one of the photos of the embracing couple. Johnson pointed out that he copied the image, not from the famous Eisenstaedt *Life* photo, but from another photograph, taken from a different angle, that was in the public domain. In addition, the sculpture was in the news in April 2012, after a driver jumped the curb with a Mercedes-Benz and slightly damaged the statue. The driver, who had been slightly dazed by medication, was not injured. The sailor's right ankle and pants leg were crumpled in; fortunately, the damage was repairable. After its removal and repair at a cost of $125,000, it was reerected in place in early December 2012 and remains one of Sarasota's most impressive pieces of public art.

St. Armands Circle

A unique shopping neighborhood is St. Armands Circle, reached by taking the John Ringling Causeway from downtown Sarasota. The property was purchased and developed by John Ringling in the early 1920s. The area was originally owned by Charles St. Amand, a homesteader who bought 132 acres on the island for a total of less than $22 in 1893. The deed to the property erroneously listed the owner as "St. Armands," and the name stuck. After the property had been bought and sold several times, John Ringling bought it in 1917 and began work on development. Some of his circus elephants assisted in hauling building materials.

Ringling envisioned a unique circular shopping area, and he donated some statues from his personal collection to decorate the intersections and the park in the center of the circle. Now totaling more than thirty, the figures continue today to overlook the heavy automobile and pedestrian traffic swirling around them. Today, the circle and surrounding streets host more than 140 small shops, selling gifts, jewelry, and clothing, together with several restaurants, including the locally famous Columbia Restaurant, founded by the family that established the Columbia Restaurant in the Ybor City district of Tampa. At present there is only one art gallery among the many retailers in St. Armands Circle and surrounding streets, Wyland Galleries.

Wyland Galleries

Located just off the circle at 314 John Ringling Boulevard is the Wyland Galleries of Sarasota, one of the group of galleries that includes the flagship Wyland Galleries in Key West and others in St. Petersburg and in Disney World in Orlando, as well as others around the United States. Continuing the maritime theme of the Wyland group, the Sarasota gallery offers a wide range of art, generally in the high price range, in the form of paintings, prints, and

Art and sculpture inside Wyland Galleries.

relatively small sculptures and ceramic decorative works.

One amazing set of decorative pieces shown at the Wyland Galleries of Sarasota are by Clarita Brinkerhoff, who adds a sparkling surface to her works of birds, animals, and fish, using coatings of chips of Swarovski crystal, to achieve what she calls "jewelry for the home." Although we especially admired one piece of a crystal-studded eagle, we decided that the price was out of our range.

Plan your visit: 314 John Ringling Boulevard, Sarasota, (941) 388-5331.

DISTRICTS AND ART CENTERS

Art Center Sarasota

About twenty blocks farther south on Tamiami Trail from the Ringling College of Art and Design, on the west side of the street, is Art Center Sarasota, with ample parking in front. The art center offers a regular schedule of art and pottery classes, as well as showing works from juried exhibitions. Outside is a sculpture garden with several creations, including a lifelike figure by Jack Dowd of an elderly gentleman sitting on a bench with a "pet" alligator curled beneath at his feet. The sculpture is titled, ironically, *Fighting Crime in Sarasota*.

The art center holds regular juried exhibitions. A national juried exhibition called *Open Season*, held in 2019–2020, was judged by Mark Ormond, former director of the Center for the Fine Arts (Perez Art Museum) in Miami. The first-place award at this exhibition went to Kathy Simon-McDonald for her image of a chalk artist completing a work on a sidewalk. After the juried competition, the

Fighting Crime in Sarasota by Jack Dowd.

submitted pieces of art were then offered for sale at the center, with prices ranging from as low as $150 to many in the $2,500–$4,500 range, with the price of *The Chalk Artist V* set at $10,000.

Plan your visit: 707 North Tamiami Trail, Sarasota, (941) 365-2032.

Towles Court Artist Colony

Most of the studios in the "colony" are open Tuesday–Saturday. A group of bungalows and a two-story shop building at Towles Court on Adams Lane (a block off US 301/Washington Boulevard, just south of Ringling Boulevard) is a self-designated art colony. In addition to several artists' residences in nearby bungalows, the main two-story structure offers working studio space to artists in a wide variety of media, including painting, pottery, jewelry, clothing art, fiber art, and weaving.

Anne Ireland graciously invited us into her studio while working and showed

us her work; she described herself as "a contemporary landscape artist and colorist." She agreed that her work reflects a blending of impressionist and abstract styles. A philosophy graduate of Bowdoin College in Maine, she also went on to earn a BFA from the Maine College

Artist Anne Ireland.

of Art. Over the period 2004–2015 her works were in some thirty gallery shows, invitational exhibitions, and juried shows in Maine; she was also awarded residency at the Studios of Key West (discussed on page 197), as well as residencies in programs in Healdsburg, California, and Stonington, Maine. She has done a couple of covers for L.L.Bean catalogs, and her art can be seen online at anneirelandart.com.

She is one of about eighteen artists with well-lit and attractive studios or galleries in the Towles Court center.

Plan your visit: 1938 Adams Lane, Sarasota, (941) 266-7318.

ARCHITECTURE

Ca' d'Zan and Ringling Estate

The curious name of the Ringling mansion, Ca' d'Zan, is Venetian dialect of Italian for "House of John." John Ringling, who had made a fortune with his circus business between the 1880s and the 1920s, planned and built the house with his wife, Mable, in the years 1924–1926. The cost of the structure was about $1.5 million, and the furnishings cost another $400,000. In the 2020s, the total cost is the equivalent of something like $27 to $28 million. Today the mansion, located near the intersection of US 41 (Tamiami Trail) and University Boulevard, fronting on Sarasota Bay, is owned by the State of Florida and is open for visitors, along with an associated art museum, a circus museum, and surrounding landscaped gardens. The house is spectacular in its décor and setting and is well worth a

visit. The lavish furnishings and interior design of the residence evoke the lifestyle of many late nineteenth-century American entrepreneurs, who assembled decorative items and art in museum-like homes.

Plan your visit: John and Mable Ringling Museum of Art, 5401 Bay Shore Road, Sarasota, (941) 359-5700.

ART COLONIES

In addition to the Towles Court "colony," there are two other neighborhoods in Sarasota that have restored buildings and shops that some Sarasotans regard as potential art colonies:

Artful Giraffe

This shop is located in a group of some ten cottages and a neighborhood with reputedly several hundred artists in the historic (1920s) neighborhood who work in wide variety of media. The homes in this neighborhood along Fruitville Road were originally funded by John Ringling to house his circus workers. The Artful Giraffe offers art and pottery classes.

Plan your visit: 1861 Fruitville Road, Sarasota, (941) 388-3700.

Burns Court

This neighborhood is part of historic Sarasota and has a number of small shops that represent a "downtown revival" more than an art colony. The Burns Court Café at 401 South Pineapple has also doubled as a gallery. The designated Burns Court Historic District has fifteen Mediterranean Revival–style bungalows, all built in the mid-1920s by the developer Owen Burns, who himself lived in the 400 block of South Pineapple Drive

NAPLES

Naples was founded in the 1880s and got its name from local promoters asserting that the mild climate and sheltered bay resembled that of Naples, Italy. Although the town was linked to the railway network in 1927 and opened to highway traffic with the Tamiami Trail (Tampa–Miami, now US 41) in 1928, development did not take off until after World War II.

Robert Rauschenberg (1925–2008)

One of the most influential and renowned American artists of the late twentieth and early twenty-first centuries was Robert Rauschenberg. From 1970 until his death in 2008, he maintained a studio in Captiva, Florida, which, under the direction of a foundation, continues to support an artist residency program there. He was inducted in the Florida Artists Hall of Fame in 1991.

Rauschenberg served in the U.S. Navy in World War II and, after the war, briefly studied in Paris and then at Black Mountain College in North Carolina. Black Mountain had gained national attention as an institution that fostered independent thinking in the arts and other fields. Among the teachers there was Joseph Albers, who had taught at the Bauhaus in Germany before the school was closed by the Nazis. After a year at Black Mountain, Rauschenberg moved to New York City and studied at the Art Students League there.

Rauschenberg's name has been associated with the development of pop art, as well as with many other art movements of the later twentieth century. However, he rejected such attempts to label his work. One of his innovations was the creation of what he called "combines," pictures that incorporated a wide variety of three-dimensional items, including "found objects." By bringing such objects physically into his work, he challenged the distinction between painting and sculpture. Some regarded his work as "neo-Dada."

His work over the decades from the 1960s into the first decade of the twenty-first century remained innovative and creative, earning him notoriety and international fame as an artist who could not be classified. His imaginative use of materials and his highly original conceptions continued to confound critics. He not only "combined" a wide variety of objects into his artworks (ranging from a stuffed goat to household appliances, to automobile parts and tires), but he also "combined" his work with artists in other fields, including dance, theater, photography, printmaking, and others. For decades, he collaborated with modern and postmodern dance groups led by Merce Cunningham, Paul Taylor, and Trisha Brown.

In 1970, he purchased property and established a studio on Captiva Island, about twenty miles south of Fort Myers. Over the decades following, he had three studios built on the property and increased the property to about twenty acres total. Today, the Robert Rauschenberg Foundation that operates the property hosts an artist-in-residence program in which a group of about eight to ten artists, poets, writers, musicians, composers, choreographers, and others are awarded a month at the site. The residency facility is closed to the public, but group tours have been arranged on a case-by-case basis.

Due to its excellent winter climate and projects that developed residential lots on canals with navigable water and access to the ocean in the 1950s, the town began to attract very prosperous residents, many of whom owned boats or yachts. By the 2010 census, the annual *median* income for a couple in Naples was over $100,000. By one estimate, the town has the second highest proportion of millionaires per capita in the United States. As a result, the small downtown is characterized by numerous shops selling luxury goods, and real estate values have remained high.

With this background, in recent decades, Naples has developed not into a traditional "art colony," where struggling and beginning artists set up their studios, but into a town where many affluent families actively support the arts. While very few beginning or unrecognized artists can afford to live in the community, the local home and office décor market for art is active and thriving. Further, the prosperous community has been lavish in supporting an endowed museum and three theater organizations that offer plays and concerts. The town's support of the fine arts has resulted not only in a major museum-and-theater complex, but in addition, more than two dozen art galleries. Several of the galleries selling at the high price range are second or third shops opened by owners originally based in affluent cities and towns in the Northeast, particularly New England.

MUSEUMS

Naples Museum of Art

The Naples Museum of Art was established in 1989. The visual arts center on Pelican Bay Boulevard, Baker Museum, is a three-story, thirty-thousand-square-foot facility with fifteen separate display galleries. The building itself features a glass dome conservatory and entrance gates designed by metal artist Albert Paley, and chandeliers and Persian-style ceiling by glass artist Dale Chihuly.

Hayes Hall is a fourteen-hundred-seat concert hall, with two associated art galleries. Both Hayes Hall and the Baker Museum are part of the Kimberly K. Querrey and Louis A. Simpson Cultural Campus, an eight-and-a-half-acre cultural center adjacent to the upscale shopping venue of Waterside Shops. Also included in the Simpson Cultural Campus is the Daniels Pavilion, a black box theater, seating 283. Querrey, Simpson, Hayes, Baker, and Daniels, whose names are all attached to the facilities, represent generous donors who made the complex possible.

Plan your visit: 5833 Pelican Bay Boulevard, Naples, (239) 597-1111.

Artis-Naples

For frequent visitors, an annual membership fee in "Artis-Naples" is offered, providing access to other arts venues in Naples, such as musical performances, and discounts on group trips to other Florida arts facilities. The museum is also part of the Museum Travel Alliance, which arranges domestic and international trips with guides.

The art display programs and theatrical and concert shows at the Artis-Naples complex change from season to season and year to year. Recent displays of paintings and other artwork have included *100 Iconic Works from the*

Exterior façade of Artis-Naples.

Permanent Collection. These include a wide variety of artists, media, and artistic movements. Selections for this program included works by Diego Rivera, Alexander Calder, and Roy Lichtenstein. The focus on American and Mexican art of the twentieth and twenty-first centuries are two of specialties of the Baker Museum.

Past exhibits in recent years show the wide variety of the Baker Museum holdings ranging over contemporary and nineteenth- and twentieth-century art. Exhibits have included works by Bryna Prensky, Philip Haas, Daniel Buren, Arik Levy, and John Carroll Long, among others.

The museum is able to offer such a wide variety because of donations of private collections to the museum over its two decades. For example, one of the benefactors of the museum was Olga

Hirshhorn, who donated her collection of some four hundred works in 2013. The Hirshhorn collection included works by Alexander Calder, Larry Rivers, and Josef Albers.

Gate to Baker Museum at Artis-Naples.

The Beach and the Cliffs of Aval by Claude Monet.

Along with her husband Joe Hirshhorn, the founding donor of the Hirshhorn Museum and Sculpture Garden in the Smithsonian complex of museums on the mall in Washington, D.C., Mrs. Hirshhorn established close friendships with internationally known artists including Pablo Picasso, Willem de Kooning, and Georgia O'Keeffe. Part of Olga Hirshhorn's unique collection of paintings and prints is commonly known to the museum curators as *The Mouse House*, consisting of small-scale works originally installed in the tiny five-hundred-square-foot home in Washington, D.C., that she purchased after her husband passed away.

The vast collection of works allows the museum to offer informative and interest-

ing displays of classic works by French impressionists and postimpressionists, among many other periods.

Generous donations by other benefactors since the founding of the museum in 1989 have enriched the collection, which of course can only display partial selections from the large numbers of acquisitions at any one time. Past donations have included the "foundational" Ahmet Ertegun Collection acquired in 2000, which includes work by historical American artists such as A. E. Gallatin, Alexander Calder, and Thomas Hart Benton. Amassed by music industry entrepreneur Ahmet Ertegun in the 1970s, the selection reflects his goals of "balanced aesthetics and content."

The Couple by José Clemente Orozco.

A major selection of modern Mexican art came from the Harry Pollak Collection acquired in 2002. The Harry Pollak Collection, put together over a period of some thirty years, includes works by Diego Rivera, José Clemente Orozco, David Alfaro Siqueiros, and Rufino Tamayo, among others. The Pollak Collection includes works by these masters of twentieth-century Mexican art and documents the development of that whole genre or style. Some of the prized items in this collection are Rufino Tamayo's *White Nude*, José Clemente

Orozco's *The Red Curtain*, and *Girl Selling Ducks* by Alfredo Zalce (which was chosen as the cover image for the guide to the Pollak Collection), as well as two works by Diego Rivera.

The museum's holdings of Mexican artists' works was enriched with the Bryna Prensky Collection, a gift by Michael F. and Tonya L. Aranda in 2007. The Prensky Collection largely consists of work by a group of emerging artists who lived and worked in Mexico in the latter half of the twentieth century. This collection includes a great diversity of

The Painter and His Muse by Marc Chagall.

styles and subject matter and reflects Bryna Prensky's efforts to establish wider recognition of aspiring artists.

Other donations of private collections over the twenty-year life of the museum have continued to enrich the possible selected offerings to the public, with gallery displays regularly changed every year.

Plan your visit: 5833 Pelican Bay Boulevard, Naples, (239) 597-1111.

GALLERIES

As noted above, there are more than twenty-four art galleries in Naples, which range from those selling very high-priced works by internationally recognized artists, to shops selling less expensive originals and prints. About twelve of the galleries are concentrated in two areas of a few blocks of the downtown, and visitors often stroll through these neighborhoods to visit these galleries and other interesting shops, where a wide variety of eateries is also clustered. One of these clusters of galleries is along Fifth Avenue South—the elegant shopping district at the heart of old Naples—and the other is about six blocks to the south of that street, in and near the Third Street South complex.

Gallery One

This gallery notes contemporary works in these categories, from more than two hundred artists: glass, wall art, sculpture, jewelry, and Judaica.

Plan your visit: 770 Fifth Avenue South, Naples, (239) 263-0835.

Shaw Gallery

One of the older galleries in Naples, in business for more than thirty-one years, the gallery offers fine art paintings, sculpture, and art glass.

Plan your visit: 761 Fifth Avenue South, Naples, (239) 251-7826.

Native Visions Gallery

This gallery shows a wide variety of African wild life art, both pictorial and sculptural. This gallery is associated with another in Jupiter, Florida.

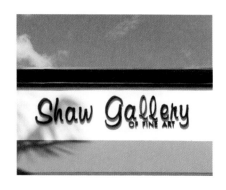

Plan your visit: 737 Fifth Avenue South, Naples, (239) 643-3785.

Emily James Gallery

This gallery displays the work of the artist Emily James, including large realistic oil paintings of seascapes. She and her husband host the shop.

Plan your visit: 720 Fifth Avenue South, Naples, (877) 454-8336.

Sheldon Fine Art

This gallery has other locations in Newport, Rhode Island, and Saratoga Springs, New York, and has been in business for more than thirty-five years.

Plan your visit: 460 Fifth Avenue South, Naples, (239) 649-6255.

Englishman Fine Art

The owner of this gallery also operates another gallery in Nuffield, Surrey, in the United Kingdom. The shop offers paintings, sculpture, furnishings, and engravings. This shop has also been in operation for more than thirty-five years.

Plan your visit: 365 Fifth Avenue South, Suite 101, Naples, (239) 649-8088.

L Modern Art Gallery

This gallery offers the work of Chinese-born L. Li. He was born in China in 1958 and, as a child, was sent to the countryside during the Cultural Revolution. He later studied at the Lu Xun Academy of Fine Art, where he later became a professor of traditional Chinese painting and sculpture. He visited the United States in 1992 and now resides in Atlanta, Georgia. The gallery specializes in his work, which combines traditional methods and contemporary styles in a very personal style. Together with his brother, he has operated galleries in Atlanta, Georgia; Columbia, South Carolina; and Orlando, Florida.

Plan your visit: 300 Fifth Avenue South, Suite 113, Naples, (239) 302-6517.

There is a cluster of galleries at the Third Street South complex (near the intersection of Third Street South and Broad Avenue South) and others nearby to the complex on Broad Avenue South. For those driving or walking the neighborhoods, this second neighborhood can be reached by turning south on Third Street from Fifth Avenue East. Broad Avenue South is about a half mile south of Fifth Avenue South. The Broad Avenue South and nearby area is sometimes referred to as Gallery Row and is the locale of some of the highest-quality galleries in the state of Florida.

Arsenault Studio and Banyan Arts Gallery

This gallery features the work of Paul Arsenault, who has lived and worked in Naples since 1974. The "Banyan" refers to the Banyan tree on the Arsenault property, where numerous artists and writers have stayed over the decades. In addition to the modern impressionist works of Paul Arsenault, the gallery also carries works by a limited number of other artists in its seven showrooms.

Plan your visit: 1199 Third Street South, Naples, (239) 263-1214.

HW Gallery

This gallery has been in business since about 2004 and features modern and contemporary art by internationally recognized artists, including Roy Lichtenstein, Andy Warhol, Robert Rauschenberg, Pablo Picasso, and others. The gallery carries new works by a limited number of contemporary artists but typically focuses on original works by artists with well-established international reputations.

Plan your visit: 1305 Third Street South, Naples, (239) 263-6640.

DeBruyne Fine Art

With more than five thousand square feet and two stories, this is the largest gallery in Naples and in all of southwest Florida.

The owners pride themselves on only showing the work of established artists, defined by having been shown in other galleries and museums. In addition to work by renowned contemporary artists, the gallery also features antique works, only after meticulous research to establish authenticity. Most of the works are impressionist or realistic, with numerous nineteenth- and early twentieth-century pieces. The striking building has many galleries within it for display of art in comfortable, museum-quality settings.

Plan your visit: 275 Broad Avenue South, Naples, (239) 262-4551.

Gardner Colby Gallery

Following a gallery established in 1994 on Martha's Vineyard, Massachusetts, established by Nancy Winch and her husband, Tony, the couple chose the Broad Avenue South location for a second location, because of its overall ambience. The gallery offers a wide range of

abstract, traditional, and coastal subjects in the higher price range. As in other galleries offering highest-quality work, the staff are happy to assist with framing, shipping, lighting, and installation.

Plan your visit: 359 Broad Avenue South, Naples, (239) 403-7787.

Quidley & Company Fine Art Gallery
This company has two other galleries, one on Nantucket Island, Massachusetts, and one in Westport, Connecticut.

Plan your visit: 375 Broad Avenue South, Naples, (239) 261-4300.

Harmon-Meek Gallery
Specializing in modern works, this is a large, two-story gallery. Harmon-Meek also has a second location at 599 Ninth Street North. This Twelfth Avenue South gallery is one of the oldest continuing art

galleries in Naples, operating since 1964. Founded by William Meek, the gallery is a family-owned business, and the shop justly lays claim to founding "Gallery Row" in the neighborhood.

Plan your visit: 382 Twelfth Avenue South, Naples, (239) 262-2699.

Phil Fisher Gallery
This is an artist-owned gallery, located near the Naples city yacht docks and a cluster of restaurants, at the east end of Twelfth Avenue South, some five blocks from the galleries clustered in the Third Street South neighborhood. The gallery features the contemporary landscape art of Phil Fisher—both local scenes and those from his travels and residencies abroad, in Italy, Mexico, the Bahamas, and elsewhere. His colorful works are in the impressionist tradition.

Phil Fisher Gallery.

Plan your visit: 810 Twelfth Avenue South, Naples, (239) 403-8393.

Most of the galleries described above tend to sell at the high end of the price and quality ranges. Scattered through other parts of Naples are other types of galleries, some of which offer more moderate pricing and framing services as well.

Adams Galleries

This five-thousand-square-foot shop offers framing services as well as art at the moderate price range, and is a relatively new location for this business, which began in 1998.

Plan your visit: 2154 Trade Center Way, Naples, (239) 403-0040.

Aldecor Custom Framing and Gallery

This is a two-story shop that sells moderate priced art and provides decorating and framing services as well.

Plan your visit: 1786 Trade Center Way, Naples, (239) 778-0663.

Art 41 Gallery

This is an artist-owned gallery selling works by Eric and Jessica Crabtree. The couple specialize in custom contemporary paintings, including seascapes, and "coastal contemporary" works.

Plan your visit: 2080 J and C Boulevard, Naples, (239) 249-2005.

Samaniego Fine Art

This gallery is artist owned, by Arturo Samaniego, who offers contemporary seascapes, among other works. The shop also sells works of emerging and midcareer artists from around the world. Admired as a teacher, Samaniego holds art classes as well.

Plan your visit: 2220 J and C Boulevard, Unit 6, Naples, (239) 431-7040.

Harmon-Meek Gallery

This is the second location of this well-established gallery, described above.

Plan your visit: 599 Ninth Street North, Suite 309, Naples, (239) 261-2637.

KAJ Gallery

In the "design district," this gallery features contemporary art, sculpture, and masks.

Plan your visit: 462 Tamiami Trail North (Ninth Street North), Naples, (239) 234-7918.

Chernysh Antiques and Fine Art

This shop buys and sells decorative items, art, and antiques.

Naples Art Association.

Plan your visit: Treasure Island Antique Mall, 950 Central Avenue, Naples, (941) 888-4226.

Kunjani Craft Coffee and Gallery
This is a coffee shop specializing in African blends of coffee and incidentally showing and selling framed art.

Plan your visit: 780 Seagate Drive, Naples, (239) 300-0196.

Vino's Picasso
This shop offers paint lessons together with wine parties in the evenings, one of several such "wine and art" shops established in recent years across the United States.

Plan your visit: Galleria Shops, 2367 Vanderbilt Beach Road, Suite 1, Naples, (239) 431-8750.

NAPLES ART ASSOCIATION

This nonprofit association, at the north end of Gambier Park, a block south of the high-end shopping district along Fifth Avenue, hosts classes and rotating shows of art in its in-house galleries.

Plan your visit: 585 Park Street, Naples, (239) 262-6517.

SOUTH ATLANTIC COAST and KEY WEST

DELRAY BEACH

Like many other small towns in Florida, Delray Beach grew out of an agricultural settlement, as the town was known as the center for pineapple farming in the early decades of the twentieth century. In the years from 1920 to 1941, the town gained repute as an art colony, with many artists and writers making their winter homes in the town. Nationally known cartoonists H. T. Webster and Fontaine Fox attracted others, including James Crossley Raymond and Denys Wortman. Largely forgotten in the present era, these artists created characters and settings that became part of the mass culture. Webster developed the character Caspar Milquetoast; Fox was known for the *Toonerville Trolley* newspaper cartoon; Raymond took over the production of the comic strip *Blondie* and developed the title character's distinctive look; Wortman depicted tragicomic scenes of street life in New York City. Better remembered today is Pulitzer Prize–winning poet Edna St. Vincent Millay, who also maintained a winter home in the town; she had lived in internationally famous art colonies of the day—Greenwich Village in New York, and in Paris.

Although the art colony national reputation of Delray Beach declined after World War II, the town now continues to attract artists, many who maintain studios and sell their works in local galleries.

MUSEUMS

Cornell Art Museum
Located on Old School Square, the Cornell Art Museum is housed in a restored elementary school building. Opened in 1990, the museum was named for local residents Harriet W. and George D. Cornell. Renovated in 2017, the building features an interior atrium that provides natural lighting to many of the exhibits. Every spring, the museum has hosted an outdoor juried art exhibition in the square, which, it is hoped, will continue in future years.

Plan your visit: 51 North Swinton Avenue, Delray Beach, (561) 243-7922.

GALLERIES

Addison Gallery
This gallery is located in the Pineapple Grove Arts District, so named because of the area's former fame as a pineapple-raising area and the present location of several galleries and artists' studios. The gallery shows both established and emerging artists. The gallery also offers art consulting services for individuals and businesses.

Plan your visit: 206 NE Second Street, Delray Beach, (561) 278-5700.

Sundook Art Galleries

Founded in 1979, Sundook features original art, fine art prints, and bronze and acrylic sculptures. The gallery offers worldwide shipping and museum-quality framing services. The gallery's collection includes many works by world-renowned contemporary artists.

Plan your visit: 524 East Atlantic Avenue, Delray Beach, (561) 266-3425.

Blue Gallery

The Blue Gallery consists of three showrooms at 600, 610, and 616 East Atlantic Avenue. All show contemporary art works; the showroom at 600 East Atlantic Avenue offers sculpture as well as paintings. On the gallery website, owner Rami Rotkopf provides thorough, detailed biographies of each of the artists whose works are on display.

Plan your visit: Old School Square, Delray Beach, (561) 265-0020.

Avalon Gallery

This shop offers glass sculptures and lamps as well as a selection of Judaica.

Plan your visit: 426 East Atlantic Avenue, Delray Beach, (561) 272-9155.

Amanda James

The gallery is operated by Amanda Johnson and James Knill, both practicing local artists. Unique works include textiles and clothing derived from Amanda Johnson's paintings, as well as photographs by James Knill, who is also an abstract expressionist painter.

Plan your visit: 400 Gulfstream Boulevard, #7, Delray Beach, (561) 270-7832.

Magnus and Gordon

Founded in 2013 by Brenda Gordon and Magnus Sebastian, this gallery features locally produced original artwork, and is proud to be part of the small but thriving group of artists on "Artist's Alley."

Plan your visit: 354 NE Fourth Street, Unit C, Delray Beach, (561) 212-6714.

Cacace Fine Art

Established in the early 1990s, Cacace Fine Art sells original oil paintings, sculptures, and prints and is one of the longest-operating galleries in the Pineapple Grove Arts District.

Plan your visit: 354 NE Fourth Street, Suite D, Delray Beach, (561) 276-1177.

COMMUNITY ART

Arts Warehouse

Located near the intersection of Third Street and Third Avenue is a community art center and "Arts Warehouse" at the end of Artist's Alley. The center opened in 2017, using a fifteen-thousand-square-foot warehouse, intended to serve as a "catalyst for economic development and growth within the Pineapple Grove Arts District and the Community Redevelopment Area." The center rents studio space; provides a gallery and exhibit space; and has space for classrooms, workshops, and special events. The Community Redevelopment Area organization hopes to enhance the community's image as an arts destination.

Plan your visit: 313 NE Third Street, Delray Beach, (561) 330-9614.

MIAMI

Compared to St. Augustine and even to Tallahassee, Miami has a short history. It was only a small settlement until Henry Flagler decided to extend his railroad line down the east coast of Florida from St. Augustine. When the Florida East Coast Railway reached Miami in 1896, the town had only fifty residents. Today, Miami and Miami Beach make up the largest metropolitan area in Florida, with more than six million residents, more than double the next largest metropolitan area in Florida, Orlando, with about two and a half million. Tallahassee, the state capital, has fewer than four hundred thousand residents, of whom a large proportion are students at local colleges or state employees. In addition to the large population of snowbirds (temporary winter residents) and retirees from the Northeast, in recent decades Miami has become more international with refugees and émigrés from the Caribbean and Latin America.

Miami is more culturally diverse than any other Florida city, with a very large Latin American population, including not only hundreds of thousands of Cubans, but sizable populations of immigrants and residents from Haiti, other Caribbean islands, and Central and South America. In addition, the city's large population includes some of the most affluent residents of Florida, including many patrons of the arts, both as collectors and attendees at art events and visitors to the area's many art museums and galleries. Due to Miami's sheer size, it is not surprising that the metro area is

Red, White, Blue & Grey Girls, Wynwood Walls mural. *Photo by Francisco Zuniga on Unsplash*

by far the largest art market or art-conscious place in Florida, as measured by the number of art museums and art galleries.

In addition to these factors that make the city a thriving market for the fine arts, since the year 2002 Miami Beach has hosted an annual art fair or art convention, which is one of the largest and most prestigious in the world: Art Basel Miami. This annual event brings thousands of collectors, art buyers, critics, gallery owners, and practicing artists to the city every December, and their influence in stimulating the local art scene is profound. By far, most of the twenty or more active art galleries that thrive in the city were established after the coming of the Art Basel shows to Miami Beach, and several of Miami's established art museums have moved to new and impressive quarters in recent years. Furthermore, as detailed below, various civic and art organizations have organized art events to coincide with the early December schedule of Art Basel Miami, so that both Miami and Miami Beach are inundated with additional tens of thousands of artists, gallery owners, art buyers, and art tourists every year.

As in other towns, several districts have become the neighborhoods where the visual arts thrive in active galleries, smaller museums, and outdoor art in the form of sculpture and murals: the Design District, the Wynwood District, and to an extent, Little Haiti, a neighborhood of Haitian refugees and émigrés.

MUSEUMS

Depending on how "affiliated" museums are counted, and taking note of the smaller museums that are devoted to a single culture, those that are located in the suburbs of Miami (Miami Beach and North Miami), as well as several private collections set up as museums, there are more than a dozen art museums in "greater Miami." In addition to long-established university art collections and historical museums, there has been a proliferation of new art museum venues since the coming of the annual Art Basel show in 2002. That annual event has vastly increased the number of art tourists and buyers to Miami; in addition, several arts districts and tourist-destination districts have succeeded in creating a climate welcoming to the arts that has contributed to the opening of new museums as well as new art galleries.

Vizcaya Museum and Gardens

This ornate mansion and grounds are the former estate of businessman James Deering, who earned his fortune with the McCormick-International Harvester Company. The estate fronts on Biscayne Bay and incorporates Italian Renaissance gardens, a portion of native woodland landscape, and a "village" of historical outbuildings. The structure and gardens were modeled on Italian Renaissance styles, designed by twentieth-century architect F. Burall Hoffman and artistic director Paul Chalfin. The estate was built in the period 1914–1922 and is one of the best and most well-preserved examples of the Mediterranean Revival in

Girl Resting, Paint Dropping, Two Hummingbirds, Wynwood Walls mural. *Photo by Bruce Warrington on Unsplash*

Florida. Many of the building's furnishings were collected in Italy.

Plan your visit: 3251 South Miami Avenue, Miami, (305) 250-9133.

Frost Art Museum, Florida International University
Florida International University hosts two separate art museums: the Frost Art Museum and the Wolfsonian Museum, noted below along with other museums located in Miami Beach. The Frost Art Museum is renowned for its Latin American art collection and its twentieth-century American art. The collection was expanded in 1989, when the Metropolitan Museum and Art Center of Coral Gables closed and transferred its collection of twenty-eight hundred items to the Frost. The vast collection was rehoused in a new building in 2008. Its

collection is supplemented by an outdoor sculpture garden containing dozens of monumental statues and sculptures, designated as the Martin Z. Marguiles Sculpture Park.

Plan your visit: 10975 SW Seventeenth Street, Miami, (305) 348-2890.

Pérez Art Museum
Located in a twenty-acre Museum Park, the Pérez is a contemporary art museum, in a 2013 building designed by Herzog and de Meuron Architects, facing the waterway. The museum's large collection includes a selection donated by Jorge Pérez, and one of the museum's great strengths is on modern and contemporary works by Latin American artists.

Plan your visit: 1103 Biscayne Boulevard, Miami, (305) 375-3000.

Institute of Contemporary Art

This museum was located for about three years in a temporary space before settling in its present permanent setting in 2017 in the Design District. The institute began in 2014, with the decision of a group of the board of the Museum of Contemporary Art in North Miami to create a separate institution. Of the nine hundred items in the North Miami museum, two hundred were selected to form the basis of the new institution in the Design District. The distinctive building with a metallic front was designed by Spanish architects Aranguen & Gallegos. The museum shows the work of local and emerging contemporary artists but also shows the works of twentieth-century greats such as Pablo Picasso. Admission is free, but tickets should be reserved in advance.

Plan your visit: 61 NE Forty-First Street, Miami, (305) 237-7770.

Museum of Art and Design at Miami Dade College (MOAD at MDC)

This museum is housed in the Freedom Tower building, originally erected in 1925 as the offices and plant of the newspaper the *Miami News*. For years, the building held the record as the tallest building in the Miami area. Beginning in the 1960s, the building became the processing center for refugees from Cuba, and it was used for that purpose until 1972. In the period 1997–2005, the tower housed a museum and monument to Cuban resistance to the Castro regime. Today there is a Cuban American museum in the building, while the second floor is devoted to the Miami Dade College

University of Miami

The University of Miami offers a BA in art with thirty-six credits in one of three tracks: studio art, art history, or "general study," which includes courses in both studio art and art history. The university also offers a BFA degree, which requires seventy-two credits. The BA requires that the student complete a minor in another field as well.

Museum of Art and Design. The focus of the museum is the relationship of art and design to contemporary social and technological issues. Miami Dade College also hosts neighborhood art displays at numerous sites throughout Dade County.

Plan your visit: 600 Biscayne Boulevard, Miami, (305) 237-7770.

Blue and Yellow Door Painted Door, Miami. *Photo by Jason Briscoe on Unsplash*

Haitian Heritage Museum

Set up in 2004 by Eveline Pierre and Serge Rodriguez, recognizing the bicentennial of Haitian independence, this gallery/museum specializes in the art and culture of Haiti. The museum's goal is to celebrate and recognize Haitian culture, music, and history, not just pictorial art. This museum is located squarely in the neighborhood known as Little Haiti in Miami.

Plan your visit: 4141 NE Second Avenue, #105C, Miami, (305) 371-5988.

North Miami Museum of Contemporary Art (MoCA)

This museum is operated by the City of North Miami and is noted for its wide variety of community outreach programs, as well as its strong holdings in modern and contemporary art. In 2014, the organization divided, with a portion of the collection and directors forming the core of the Institute of Contemporary Art in the Design District, as noted above.

Plan your visit: 770 NE 125th Street, Miami, (805) 893-6211.

Bass Museum of Art

The focus of this museum is on international contemporary art, including design, fashion, and architecture. The museum seeks to represent the local diverse cultural context of Miami Beach.

Plan your visit: 2100 Collins Avenue, Miami Beach, (305) 673-7530.

Jewish Museum of Florida

The museum is affiliated with Florida International University and is located in two separate buildings. Its premier exhibit consists of documentation of five hundred years of Jewish life in Florida, presented through photographs, art, and artifacts. The collection consists of more than one hundred thousand items that relate to the Jewish heritage in Florida.

Plan your visit: 301 and 311 Washington Avenue, Miami Beach, (305) 672-5044.

Wolfsonian—Florida International University

The Wolfsonian museum is located in the Art Deco District of Miami Beach and houses two collections that focus on the period from 1885 to 1945. The collections go well beyond the usual conception of what a fine art museum might display, to include rare books, works in ceramics and metal, furnishings, textiles, medals, and items of industrial design.

Plan your visit: 1001 Washington Avenue, Miami Beach, (305) 531-1001.

de la Cruz: Private Collection

The de la Cruz Collection is in the heart of the Miami Design District, owned by the Cuban-born American businessman Carlos de la Cruz and his wife, Rosa. It houses their art collection and is open to the public free of charge.

Plan your visit: 23 NE Forty-First Street, Miami, (305) 576-6112.

The Margulies: Private Collection

This collection consists of contemporary and vintage photography, video, and sculpture displayed in a huge converted-warehouse space. This is another family collection established as a museum for the public.

Plan your visit: The Warehouse, 591 NW Twenty-Seventh Street, Miami, (305) 576-1051.

Weird figures with tree & metal door, Miami mural. *Photo by Juan Carlos Trujillo on Unsplash*

Rubell Family Collection: Private Collection
This museum opened in its present location in Wynwood late in 2019 and is based on a family-owned private collection of contemporary works.

Plan your visit: 1100 NW Twenty-Third Street, Miami, (305) 573-6090.

Juan Carlos Maldonado Art Collection: Private Collection
This formerly private collection emphasizes Latin American art from the 1930s to the 1970s and also includes contemporary North American works.

Plan your visit: Design District, 3841 NE Second Avenue, Suite 201, Miami, (305) 456-6126.

Girl in Rain mural. *Photo by Cooper Dan Kitchener on Unsplash*

GALLERIES: DESIGN DISTRICT

Miami has more art galleries than any other town or city in Florida, with at least twenty in business early in the year 2020. Only three predate the arrival of Art Basel in the year 2002. The three older galleries are Bakehouse, Rosenbaum, and Locust; descriptions are provided below.

The Design District hosts many of the Miami galleries and, in addition to the following art galleries, has many high-end shops devoted to the most familiar and expensive lines of clothing, jewelry, and shoes, such as Hermes, Gucci, and Prada. An open walkway at the Palm Court Shopping Center, at 140 NE Thirty-Ninth Street, culminates in a plaza that encircles a twelve-foot-diameter replica of a Buckminster Fuller sculpture, *Fly's Eye Dome*, which was installed in 2011. The Design District is roughly bounded by NE Thirty-Ninth Street to NE Forty-First Street and Biscayne Boulevard Way to NE Second Avenue.

Because of the very active market for art in Miami, and due to the vicissitudes of the economy, the number and location of art galleries in the city is subject to change. This list reflects nearly all the galleries open in early 2020, but the status of any particular gallery, as well as its hours of operation, should be verified in advance by phone.

Opera Gallery

This is a chain or group of twelve galleries worldwide in prestigious locations, originally founded in 1994. The gallery focuses on modern and contemporary artists and has two locations in the Design District.

Plan your visit: Design District, 151 NE 151st Street, Suite 131, and 140 NE Forty-First Street, Miami, (305) 868-3337.

Barred Window with Graffiti, graffiti art, Miami. *Photo by Harishi Kabalasingam on Unsplash*

Kavachnina Contemporary Art

This gallery was established in 2009 by Gala Kavachnina. She has developed personal relations with both artists and collectors and has worked to attract both young and well-established artists. She works to identify artists who have unique or exceptional technique, style, and subject matter.

Plan your visit: 201 North Forty-Sixth Street, Miami, (786) 355-4394.

Avant Gallery

Founded in 2007, the Avant Gallery shows both established artists and those early in their careers. The gallery has other locations—one in Dubai, and the original Avant Gallery in New York City at the Shops at Hudson Yards.

Plan your visit: Epic Hotel, 720 Biscayne Boulevard Way, #120, Miami, (786) 220-8600.

Bakehouse Art Complex

This cooperative gallery was founded in 1985, and set up in an art deco–style former bakery on a 2.3-acre "campus." The gallery includes studio-residences for artists and shows the work of about one hundred resident and associate artists in two galleries. The artists work in a wide variety of media that include not only painting and multimedia wall art, but also photography, ceramics, woodworking, and welded metal. This is one of the three Miami galleries that predate the Art Basel shows in Miami Beach.

Plan your visit: 561 NW Thirty-Second Street, Miami, (305) 576-2828.

Markowicz Fine Art

Established in 2010, this gallery displays the works of established international artists, as well as exceptional emerging artists. For example, the gallery is the exclusive agent to the French artist Alain Godon, who has developed a technique of deconstructing his work and reproducing variations of it that he has dubbed "bildoreliefo." Markowicz also operates a gallery in Dallas, Texas.

Plan your visit: 110 NE Fortieth Street, Miami, (786) 615-8158.

Maman Fine Art

With another shop located in Buenos Aires, Argentina, Maman Fine Art focuses on Latin American (especially Argentine) art and contemporary art. The gallery in Miami opened in 2013 and has sought to establish a reputation as the "epicenter" for modern and contemporary Latin American art in Miami.

Plan your visit: 3930 NE Second Avenue, #204, Miami, (305) 571-3522.

Locust Project

This gallery was set up in 1998, with a goal of providing a noncommercial outlet for local artists. This is one of the three Miami galleries that predates the establishment of Art Basel Miami.

Plan your visit: 3852 North Miami Avenue, Miami, (305) 576-8570.

Art Angels

Jacqueline Napal and Kat Emery set up this gallery, which is by appointment only, in 2013.

Plan your visit: 127 NE Fortieth Street, Miami, (786) 753-8088.

Mora Studio

Enrique Mora, with another shop in San Juan, Puerto Rico, is an artist with an international reputation. He has produced landscapes from Latin America, Asia, and the United States. His gallery in Miami is also his personal studio, unique among Miami galleries in housing a working artist-owner.

Plan your visit: 66 NE Fortieth Street, Miami, (904) 382-4582.

Rosenbaum Contemporary Gallery

This is a "Miami branch" of a family-owned gallery originally based in Boca Raton and has operated in Miami since 1979. The owners maintain a mixed inventory of "paintings, photographs, sculptures, works on paper and mixed media pieces" including works by well-known modern and contemporary artists. The Rosenbaums also offer acquisition advice and consulting services to collectors and businesses. This is the oldest of the three galleries that predate Miami Art Basel.

Plan your visit: 140 NE Thirty-Ninth Street, Suite PC102, Miami, (786) 899-0676.

Swampspace Gallery

This gallery was established in 2005 by prolific local artist Oliver Sanchez. It is another of the very few artist-owned, artist-operated galleries in Miami.

Plan your visit: 3940 North Miami Avenue, Miami, (305) 710-8631.

GALLERIES: WYNWOOD DISTRICT

A second gallery district or neighborhood is located to the south of the Design

Pink and Blue Steel Gate, Wynwood Gate. *Photo by Jason Briscoe on Unsplash*

District and is a fifty-block neighborhood roughly bounded on the north and south by NW Twenty-Ninth Street and NW Twentieth Street, and by North Miami Avenue on the east and the I-95 interstate on the west. The whole neighborhood is characterized by more than two hundred murals (many in "graffiti" style), anchored by a courtyard of murals known as "Wynwood Walls" at 2520 NW Second Avenue.

In the mid- and late twentieth century, the neighborhood had been an enclave for Caribbean immigrants, as well as the center of Miami's Garment District, with numerous factories and workshops. The neighborhood severely declined in the 1990s, but in the early 2000s, a few developers and property owners began rehabilitating warehouses, factories, and other buildings. Following the 2002 establishment of Art Basel, the neighborhood hosted the establishment of several galleries, and a wide variety of young entrepreneurs established new businesses of other kinds in the district.

Formerly the neighborhood hosted numerous galleries, but in 2020, there are just a few remaining.

Gary Nader Art Center

After operating the Nader Gallery in Santo Domingo, Dominican Republic, beginning in 1981, Gary Nader moved to Miami in 1985, specializing in Latin American art. He established another gallery in Coral Gables in 1992. Now his Miami operation consists of fifty-five thousand square feet of exhibition space, divided among three areas: Gary Nader Private Collection, Exhibition Gallery, and Sculpture Garden. He shows not only modern and contemporary works, but also works by impressionists like Manet and Monet, and early twentieth-century greats such as Pablo Picasso, Andy Warhol, and Marc Chagall.

Plan your visit: 62 NE Twenty-Seventh Street, Miami, (305) 576-0256.

Projects Gallery
Plan your visit: 250 NW Twenty-Third Street, Miami, (267) 303-9652.

Oliver Cole Gallery

Oliver Cole has been active in what his website describes as the "art industry" for more than two decades. After spending eight years in New York City working on curatorial projects, he opened his first gallery in Miami in 2004. He began the present operation in 2015, showing modern and contemporary works.

Plan your visit: 301 NW Twenty-Eighth Street, Miami, (305) 392-0179.

GALLERIES: LITTLE HAITI DISTRICT

A third neighborhood or district with several galleries and other art-related businesses is Little Haiti. This neighborhood is anchored by the Caribbean Marketplace at 5935 NE Second Avenue, and extending from about NE Sixty-Fifth Street to NE Fifty-Ninth Street between NE Second Avenue and NE Fourth Avenue.

N'Namdi Contemporary Fine Art

This gallery was founded in 2012. Jumaane N'Namdi has operated a gallery in Detroit since 1981, as well as others in New York and Chicago for shorter periods. He has worked with the Art Institute of Chicago, the Detroit Institute of Arts, the Perez Art Museum Miami, the Smithsonian, and the Studio Museum of Harlem, among others.

Plan your visit: 6505 NE Second Street, Miami, (766) 332-4736.

Emerson Dorsch

This gallery is operated by the husband-and-wife team of Brook Dorsch and Tyler Emerson-Dorsch. Tyler Emerson-Dorsch joined her husband in operating the gallery in 2008 after earning a master's degree from the Center for Curatorial Studies at Bard College in New York State. The gallery has had several locations in Miami over more than two decades, before choosing the Little Haiti location. The gallery represents south Florida–based emerging and midcareer artists.

Plan your visit: 5900 NW Second Avenue, Miami, (305) 576-1278.

Nina Johnson

The Nina Johnson gallery is a "contemporary art space." Since 2007, the gallery has produced exhibitions by emerging and established artists from around the world.

Plan your visit: 6315 NW Second Avenue, Miami, (305) 571-2288.

Yeelen Group

This art brokerage firm is headed by attorney Karla Ferguson. Born in Kingston, Jamaica, she holds degrees in political science and international relations from Florida International University, in international business transactions from La Sorbonne in Paris, and a law degree from Tulane University. She has curated contemporary art exhibitions.

Plan your visit: 294 NW Fifty-Fourth Street, Miami, (305) 742-5428.

ART BASEL MIAMI

An annual event in Miami since the year 2002 has been the Art Basel show that is held in early December. The idea for the event, as well as its name, traces back to the late 1960s, when three gallery owners from Basel, Switzerland, joined forces. The Basel gallery owners—Trudi Bruckner, Balz Hilt, and Ernst Beyeler— had attended a German 1967 art show in Cologne, Germany, and decided that they could improve on it by setting up an international art show in their home city of Basel. Basel is ideally located for international meetings, on the northwestern edge of Switzerland, at the point where the borders of France, Germany, and Switzerland converge.

Graffiti images at sidewalk level, graffiti art, Miami. *Photo by Haus of Zero on Unsplash*

That first Art Basel show in Switzerland in 1970 drew ninety galleries and thirty publishers from ten countries and more than sixteen thousand visitors. Held annually thereafter, the show continued to grow and attract visitors to Basel. By the mid-1970s, the art show in Basel drew three hundred exhibitors from twenty-one countries. In the year 2002, Art Basel arranged the first of its shows in the United States and in Hong Kong. The Miami Beach show hosted 160 galleries from twenty-three countries. In addition to the gallery displays, the show featured "Conversations," which were panel discussions with leading art figures regarding subjects such as collecting principles and how art can best be exhibited. Panel members included not only artists and art collectors, but also such professionals as art critics, curators, and museum directors.

The international Art Basel shows, held annually now in Basel, in Miami, and in Hong Kong, are presently owned by "MCH," a well-established marketing company based in Basel that organizes and sets up about ninety other events around the world, including a major watch and jewelry show. MCH is one of the world's most successful exhibition companies in terms of total volume of sales and has its historical origins in the "Swiss Sample Fair" (*Schweizer Mustermess*), first held in Basel in 1916. Through mergers and acquisitions, MCH has a role or part holding in other events including, since 2016 the India Art Fair, and since 2017 a major art show in Dusseldorf, the "fashion capital" of Germany, as well as a majority holding in an annual London art show called Masterpiece London, Limited. In addition, MCH owns several exhibition sites in Switzerland. The annual art show held in June in the "Messe Basel" (Basel Fair) structure in Switzerland continues to draw crowds of more than ninety thousand visitors.

Lorenzo Rudolf served as director of Art Basel from 1991 to 2000. He replaced the earlier gallery selection committee that had representatives from thirty countries, setting up a three-person committee that established more strict standards for selection of galleries and art. In 1995, Rudolf appointed Sam Keller as communications director, and in the year 2000, Keller became the overall director of Art Basel, on Rudolf's retirement. It was Keller who set up the first Art Basel show abroad, with Art Basel Miami Beach, in 2002, an idea that Rudolf had advocated as way to attract artists, collectors, and galleries from the United States and Latin America. Sam Keller had a genius for promotion, and from its beginnings, Art Basel Miami was a success. With the acquisition of ArtHK, and converting it to Art Basel Hong Kong, in 2012 Art Basel became not just an art-show company, but also an international brand in itself, with the three major art shows on three continents.

Observers of the art scene in Miami credit Art Basel for invigorating the art market in Miami, making the city the host of more successful art galleries and art museums than any other city or town in Florida. By 2019, Art Basel, held in the Miami Beach Convention Center, attracted more than 270 galleries, showing the work of more

Alligator mural, Miami. *Photo by Eric Christian King on Unsplash*

than four thousand artists, and hosting more than eighty thousand visitors. Miami's Art Basel shows have several special features besides gallery-sponsored booths. "Survey" includes solo shows by artists, to select galleries offering thematic exhibitions. "Art Nova" is dedicated to new works from emerging artists and new galleries. "Kabinett" shows works by a single artist or works reflecting a theme in separate booth spaces. And, continuing a feature from earlier years, "Conversations" continue to offer a variety of lectures, panel discussions, and other presentations more typical of professional or academic conferences than shows. Another feature introduced in 2019 was an outdoor installation of sculpture.

Art Basel has become such an integral part of the Miami and Miami Beach art scene that a large number of independent art events held during the same period in early December and have become known as part of "Art Basel Miami," even though they are not affiliated with the Swiss company–sponsored show at the convention center.

These satellite or independent events include about twenty local art fairs with more than twelve hundred participating galleries. Specific events include two in Miami Beach:

Scope—Miami Beach

This outdoor show focuses on the work of contemporary and "street" artists, held on the Miami Beach boardwalk. The 2019

Mural of Salvador Dali, Miami. *Photo by Juan Carlos Trujillo on Unsplash*

show had 134 exhibitors with a focus on "The New Contemporary," a genre that attempts to make critical contributions to large social and political issues.

Plan your visit: Pavilion on the Sands of Ocean Drive and Eighth Street, Miami Beach.

Design Miami

Held in tent space at Miami Beach, Design Miami hosts about three dozen international galleries that specialize in the "decorative arts." Top galleries from around the world present collectible and museum-quality exhibits of twentieth- and twenty-first-century lighting, furniture, and objets d'art.

*   *   *

In addition to these events in Miami Beach, mainland Miami also hosts a variety of art events during the "Art Basel" week, also known as the "Miami Art Week." A partial listing includes the following:

NADA Art Fair

NADA is the New Art Dealers Alliance. This fair is intended to show the works of emerging artists. The show is held at various venues; in 2019 it was at the Deauville Hotel.

Plan your visit: 1400 North Miami Avenue, Miami, (212) 594-0883.

Spectrum

Held in "Mana," in the Wynwood section of Miami at 318 NW Twenty-Third Street, this is a contemporary art show that has operated since 2010. This show brings in international artists and features "meet the artist sessions," as well as music and entertainment.

A related event is "Red Dot Miami," another contemporary art show at Mana-Wynwood, a one-hundred-thousand-square-foot event hall and a forty-thousand-square-foot sound stadium hall. These vast spaces are located in a former RC Cola manufacturing plant, now highly decorated with outdoor murals.

Plan your visit: Mana Winwood, 318 NW Twenty-Third Street, Miami.

Pinta Miami

In operation since 2006, this curated art show specializes in works from Latin America, Spain, and Portugal. The 2019

Yellow Fire Hydrant, Miami. *Photo by Ussama Azam on Unsplash*

show was also held in Mana, in Wynwood, and was set up so that some of the "Latin" galleries could show the works of artists in "solo galleries" dedicated to the works of a single artist.

Plan your visit: Mana Wynwood Convention Center, 2217 NW Fifth Avenue, Miami, (786) 514-0301.

Context Art Miami

This event began in 2012 and is intended to "create a meaningful dialogue between artists, galleries, and collectors." It is conceived as a "platform" for midcareer and emerging artists and for both new and established galleries. The 2019 Context show was held in a pavilion at One Herald Plaza.

Plan your visit: One Herald Plaza (Biscayne Bay and Fourteenth Street), Miami, (305) 517-7977.

The variety of venues and satellite fairs changes from year to year. Since serious art collectors, galleries, museums, and art tourists numbering in the tens of thousands gather in Miami and Miami Beach during the Art Basel Week (more properly known as "Miami Art Week"), travelers should be aware to book hotel, motel, or motor home or trailer space well in advance.

KEY WEST

From 1821 when the United States acquired Florida, until 1913, Key West was an extremely remote outpost, reachable only by sea. The island and city at the end of the string of keys stretching southwest from the tip of Florida were strategically located, however, facing the straits between the United States and Cuba. For this reason, the United States established both a naval base and an army fort there. During the Civil War (1861–1865), although Florida seceded from the Union and joined the Confederacy, Key West remained in Union hands. The U.S. government blockade of the ports of Florida and the Gulf coast was maintained by U.S. Naval ships based in Key West, and troops at Fort Zachary Taylor ensured federal control over Key West.

Key West is not only the oldest continuing art colony in Florida, it is one of the largest, when measured in such figures as numbers of galleries or numbers of resident local artists. Several factors have contributed to the town's attraction to artists over the decades. In common with other early art colonies, it had a reputation for being remote yet accessible, scenic, with a climate and surroundings well suited to the plein air movement that continued to attract artists ever since the movement began in France in the 1860s and 1870s. Further, the semitropical environment of Key West provided an echo of the exotic scenes that had attracted artists like Paul Gauguin in the late nineteenth century. The presence of a few well-known writers, especially Ernest Hemingway, in the 1930s helped establish the town as a refuge for unconventional and creative individuals.

ORIGINS OF KEY WEST

After the Civil War, the town benefited from a series of financial ventures, including sponge and turtle businesses, pineapple farms, and, in the 1880s

Custom House. The dancing couple in front of the Custom House Museum in Key West was sculpted by Seward Johnson.

and 1890s, the making of cigars using Cuban tobacco. In the first decade of the twentieth century, railroad entrepreneur Henry Flagler (who had earned a fortune as the financial officer of John D. Rockefeller's Standard Oil Company) oversaw the construction of rail lines linking the growing national rail network to St. Augustine in northeast Florida. Through the first decade of the twentieth century, Flagler pushed his railroad on to Miami, leading to the opening of that sleepy, out-of-the-way beach town to its first major development.

With the construction of the Panama Canal in 1904–1914, Flagler envisioned a grand plan. Key West was the U.S. port closest to Panama and already hosted both Fort Zachary Taylor and the U.S. Naval base and "coaling station" for the navy's coal-fueled warships. A rail link to Key West would allow shipment of coal to the navy at Key West by railroad tracks and bridges across the chain of keys, a stretch of about 128 miles. Furthermore, Flagler envisioned that the rail link would carry tourists "across the sea" to the semitropical, isolated town of Key West at the end of the line.

Flagler's "Florida over-the-sea railway" took seven years to complete, as the four-thousand-man workforce faced hurricanes and difficult bridge construction linking the islands. On January 22, 1912, Flagler rode the first train into Key West, less than two years before his death. The line was never very profitable, but it operated until 1935, when a hurricane (not named in those days) on Labor Day in 1935 washed out bridges, drowned hundreds of workers, and shut down the line. After negotiations, the railroad company sold the line, with its right of way and some standing bridges, to the State of Florida, and US Highway 1 opened to Key West in 1938. The rail line had already brought some development to Key West during its two decades of operation, and the town had seen modernization in the 1920s, but the destruction of the rail line, the stock market crash of 1929, and the ensuing Great Depression cut off tourism, bankrupted the local government, and cut the population of Key West in half, down to thirteen thousand by 1934. Estimates of local unemployment ran as high as 80 percent. The trip out to Key West became even more arduous after the Labor Day hurricane of 1935, with ferries linking the gaps in the highway.

Faced with a bankrupt town treasury, the loss of tourists, and disastrous unemployment, local leaders asked that the State of Florida declare a state of emergency in Key West and asked for federal assistance.

ERNEST HEMINGWAY

In the immediate aftermath of World War I, numerous American writers and artists had moved abroad, many settling in Paris. The expatriate intellectuals sought escape from both Prohibition and what they saw as the domination of American culture by conservative and "puritan" values. Some of the expatriates began returning in

Hemingway House. Ernest Hemingway lived here in the 1930s, contributing to Key West's reputation as an art colony.

the late 1920s and early 1930s. Among those was Ernest Hemingway, who sailed from France to Cuba and then took the ferry from Havana to Key West in 1928. He and his second wife, Pauline, hoped to pick up a car purchased for them by Pauline's uncle, but they found the car delivery had been delayed. Staying on, they rented an apartment at 314 Simonton Street, a building that now houses a souvenir shop.

Among literary circles, Hemingway was already well known, but few in Key West had ever heard of him. He soon took up with a group of drinking friends, including a fisherman named Joe Russell, who operated a fishing charter boat and a local speakeasy. Hemingway nicknamed him "Sloppy Joe," and the name stuck, still reflected in the name of a bar and eatery on Duval Street. The original Sloppy Joe's is now Tony's Saloon.

Over the next few years, Hemingway visited Key West. In 1931, Pauline's uncle bought the couple a house at 907 Whitehead Street that had originally been built in 1851. During remodeling, Hemingway worked in an upstairs studio in the back, writing *Death in the Afternoon*, his "bullfight" novel. Today the house is a major tourist attraction and a memorial to the author.

KEY WEST IN THE NEW DEAL

In response to the local crisis brought on by the Great Depression and pleas for federal help, the New Deal agency, the Federal Emergency Relief Agency (FERA), undertook to directly manage Key West government and address the town's financial problems. The local FERA administrator was Julius Stone Jr., an energetic and imaginative "New Dealer." Stone came up with some unusual methods, enrolling volunteers and hiring unemployed to get the city back on its feet. With a fund reputed to be about $1 million, Stone recruited workers to fix up abandoned buildings and work to make the city a tourist attraction. Garbage was collected and dumped at sea; small homes were remodeled and rented; a sewer system replaced the scattered outhouses and septic tanks. Stone encouraged even federal employees to wear bermuda shorts to work, an unheard-of informality in those times. By 1939–1940, the plan was beginning to work, with unemployment falling.

One of Stone's measures was to direct funds from the Federal Arts Projects to local artists, and the small local art colony began to flourish. A federally funded art center was established, and unemployed artists were recruited to work for a weekly federal wage of $24. The arts projects were not unique to Key West—an estimated six thousand artists across the United States got funding through the federal program, and the federal government funded about one hundred "arts centers" in large and small towns.

The combination of focused help for artists, together with the revitalization of the town, characterized the emergence of Key West as a federally supported art colony. The present-day Key West Art Center opened in 1960, and it is presumed to be the heir to the earlier, federal WPA center at the original location at 301 Front Street.

Among the many artists who benefited under the auspices of the federal program was the muralist Alfred Crimi. Two of his murals in the Key West Aquarium reflect the social realism that characterized many New Deal–funded murals around the United States. Over the years the murals were damaged, but the restorations at the aquarium reflect Crimi's original style.

One local artist who achieved lasting renown was Mario Sanchez (1908–2005), a Cuban American painter. Many of the Sanchez paintings and representations of local Hispanic life in Key West were reproduced and are still found throughout displays in such locales as the East Martello Tower and the Custom House Museum; reproductions can still be purchased at moderate prices. Many of the works of Mario Sanchez were painted in the decades from 1947 through the 1970s and 1980s, based on his memories of conditions and local scenes in Key West in earlier years, including the 1920s and 1930s.

JIMMY BUFFETT AND MARGARITAVILLE

Over the decades since World War II, Key West continued to attract artists, retirees, and others who sought escape from more conventional communities. Among the more well known of such seekers after freedom from conformity was Jimmy

Margaritaville sign. The original Margaritaville restaurant in Key West continues to draw visitors.

Buffett, who lived in Key West in the early 1980s. After earning fame as a recording artist, writer, and entrepreneur, he established the first of his "Margaritaville" restaurants in Key West in 1985.

Buffett's widely imitated "beach bum" musical style, which he dubbed "gulf and western," gave voice to a laid-back persona that launched him on a highly successful career as a musician, author, and businessman. Buffett's genius was his ability to reflect the Key West lifestyle, building a Margaritaville-themed chain of some fourteen resort hotels by the year 2020, with eleven more planned, along with more than thirty restaurants. The franchise extends through the United States, the Caribbean, Latin America, Australia, and Canada. The original 1985 Margaritaville restaurant at 516 Duval Street is now at the heart of the town's art gallery row, and remains as a monument to the international "export" of the Key West spirit.

Some may find ironies here. Key West has earned a reputation as a refuge for individualistic rebels against conformity and the sometimes stifling cultures of big business and big government. Yet the town had been connected by overseas rail to the mainland by the vision of Henry Flagler, a leading American oil and railroad capitalist of the first decades of the twentieth century. Further, the town was formally established as an art colony by Julius Stone, an agent of the federal government, in the 1930s. Its free-spirit, individualistic ethos has now become the basis for a multimillion-dollar international corporate enterprise created by Jimmy

Buffett. But of course, such ironies are found throughout cultural history.

By the 1960s, the reputation of Key West as a refuge for writers, artists, musicians, and nonconformists had become well established. It had earned its place in American imagination as a rival to New York City's Greenwich Village; Taos, New Mexico; Carmel and Big Sur in California; and towns like New Hope, Pennsylvania, and Provincetown, Massachusetts. In the present time, as measured by the number of resident artists and the number of art galleries, it is one of the largest and most successful of Florida's many art colonies, arts districts, and other types of "creative communities."

MUSEUMS

Audubon House Museum

Although the reputation of Key West as an art colony was established in the 1930s, the town's tropical location and its "exotic" tropical bird life and plants had attracted artists from much earlier in the town's existence. One of those was the great naturalist and artist James Audubon (1785–1851).

Audubon visited Key West in 1832, staying aboard ship, and exploring ashore, identifying and painting birds. He visited the home of Dr. Benjamin Strobel, an amateur ornithologist. The neighbor's house was that of Captain John Geiger, the official Key West harbor pilot, who had planted his garden with a variety of exotic plants from nearby islands in the Florida Keys and the West Indies. In his records, Audubon specifically noted that his assistant, George Lehman, painted the flowering cordia or "Geiger

Tree" as the setting for Audubon's own painting of the white-crowned pigeon. That was one of 435 illustrations that appeared in his *Birds of North America*, published in the years 1827–1838. Widely recognized as a major early nineteenth-century work of both natural science and art, the work influenced both fields for generations to come.

Although Audubon had not stayed or visited in the Geiger home in Key West, that building became locally known as the Audubon House. In the twentieth century, efforts to preserve the Geiger home as the Audubon House received funding and local support. Today the house is a handsome museum, with displays describing Audubon's visit, copies of his paintings, and some surviving flowering cordia trees in front, as well as a quiet and sheltered back garden.

As an artist, Audubon usually worked with watercolor, sometimes adding colored chalk or pastel in the "gouache" technique to soften the appearance of feathers. A careful and precisely accurate recorder of the birds of North America, Audubon became internationally recognized as a great artist as well as major naturalist of the early nineteenth century, documenting birds with his striking bird portrayals across the early United States. His depictions of tropical birds in the semitropical foliage of Florida would influence and provide inspiration for generations of later Florida artists who sought to represent the natural environment of the territory and state.

Plan your visit: 205 Whitehead Street, Key West, (305) 294-2116.

Custom House Museum and East Martello Tower

This large museum is on the next block south from the Key West Art Center. The large, red-brick "Richardsonian"-style building was originally the Key West Custom House and U.S. Post Office, opened in 1891. This museum has the definitive collection of Mario Sanchez. Some of his work is reproduced on cards and is displayed elsewhere in Key West, for example, in the Wall Warehouse.

Along with the Lighthouse Museum and the East Martello Tower, this museum is operated by the Key West Art and Historical Society. The Custom House building itself is representative of 1890s municipal architecture in the "Richardsonian Romanesque" brick style. Henry Hobson Richardson designed many public buildings in the United States over the years 1871–1886. His style was emulated by many other architects, including Key West resident William Kerr, who designed the Custom House. Like others in the Richardsonian style, the Kerr-designed custom house used a massive brick façade that evoked an almost medieval look.

The museum has displays related to the Cuban revolution against Spanish rule in the 1890s, as well as others showing the history of Key West, including the town's evolution as an artists' and writers' colony in later years. For visitors seeking to know more about the history of Key West as an art colony, this museum is very informative.

In front of the Custom House building is an impressive and much-photographed statue of a dancing couple by Seward Johnson, who has other sculptures scattered through the town and dozens more around the United States, including the massive *Unconditional Surrender* in Sarasota. The imposing statue in front of the Key West museum was donated by the sculptor, whose other sculptures include a group at the Key West lighthouse, another of five dancing nude women, and one of an artist at an easel. Near the Custom House Museum, visitors are surprised by a very lifelike statue of two ladies resting on a park bench taking a break from shopping.

Many of Johnson's sculptures are displayed in public places around the world, with more than 250 in total. They are found in Rockefeller Center, New York; in Portland, Oregon; and in Sydney, Australia. There are at least sixteen Johnson sculptures in Carmel, California.

Plan your visit: Key West Museum of Art and History at the Custom House, 281 Front Street, Key West, (305) 295-6616.

East Martello Tower
One of the Civil War–era forts in Key West, the East Martello Tower, is a combination historical and art museum, operated by the Key West Art and Historical Society. The building, one of two "Martello towers" in Key West, encloses a gun tower, where guns could be mounted to point in any direction, intended as part of the defense of the city. The museum contains a number of odd exhibits, including a "haunted doll"

Sculpture of artist. Seward Johnson caught the spirit of the plein air artists in this Key West sculpture.

as well as artifacts from the Civil War period. The tower in the central courtyard contains a permanent exhibit of the work of a local sculptor, Stanley Papio (1914–1982), known as the "junkyard rebel." Papio had earned the enmity of some of his neighbors by decorating his yard with large sculptures constructed from abandoned or junked metal pieces, including auto parts, piping, kitchen appliances, and the like. At his home on Key Largo on Highway 1 on the approach to Key West, he maintained a museum, charging 25 cents admission. He was jailed some six times for violations of court orders to clean up his "junk."

Although many locals scorned his creativity, his work drew national and international attention as art before his death at age sixty-seven.

Plan your visit: 3601 South Roosevelt Boulevard, Key West, (305) 296-3913.

STUDIO TOURS

In recent years, annual studio tours in Key West have been arranged for groups to visit four or more artists' studios with a limited group signing up in advance for the annual March tours.

Plan your visit: For information about the tours, call (305) 296-0458.

Sculpture from East Martello Tower. The definitive collection of sculptures by the "junkyard rebel," Stanley Papio, is found in Key West's East Martello Tower.

GALLERIES: DUVAL STREET—400 BLOCK

The number of galleries selling art and museums displaying art in Key West changes from year to year, as some new shops join the group already there and as some close. However, the following nineteen galleries and museums were in business in early 2020. For convenience in finding them, they are arranged in two groups; eleven on Key West's "main street," that is, Duval Street, and a separate group of eight listed as "off the beaten path."

De la Gallery

This is a one-person gallery, exclusively representing the work of Jorge de la Torriente, who produces fine seascape and landscape paintings.

Plan your visit: 419 Duval Street, Key West, (305) 395-2210.

GALLERIES: DUVAL STREET—500 BLOCK

Anna Sweet Gallery

This is another artist-owned one-person gallery, featuring the works of Anna Sweet. Her works include large-format, bright-color photographs of nude young women usually submerged in clear water, in a series called *Babes and Waves*.

Plan your visit: 513 Duval Street, Key West, (305) 916-0578.

Peter Lik Key West

This one-man shop owned by Peter Lik presents his photographic art.

Plan your visit: 519 Duval Street, Key West, (305) 292-2550.

James Coleman Gallery

James Coleman is an internationally known painter whose contemporary-impressionist works often include representations of emerging light from within a building or from the sun in a forested or urban setting; his themes also include elements from his background as a Disney artist. Many of his giclée numbered prints are moderately priced. Coleman has several other galleries across the United States.

Plan your visit: 534 Duval Street, Key West, (305) 294-7900.

GALLERIES: DUVAL STREET—600 BLOCK

Key West Gallery

This gallery shows the work of more than forty artists, mostly in residence locally.

Plan your visit: 601 Duval Street, Key West, (305) 292-9339.

Zazoo Fine Art Gallery

This gallery is owned and operated by Don Oriolo, self-described as "owner and resident artist." Oriolo has had a long career in the art, music, television, and film industries. Don's father was Joe Oriolo, who shared in the creation of the cartoon character Felix the Cat. Don inherited the franchise for Felix on his father's death in 1985. Since then, Don has established several licensing and marketing strategies for the cartoon cat, spreading the franchise to movies, video games, and television. Don Oriolo has also published several books of Felix the Cat paintings. Don can often be found at work at the gallery, which also serves as his studio.

Plan your visit: 622 Duval Street, Key West, (305) 294-8925.

Wyland Galleries

Robert Wyland is internationally known for his seascapes and large outdoor murals of whales and other sea life in ocean settings, with more than sixty murals around the world. He operates several galleries in the United States. These include five galleries in Florida, three in Hawaii, three in California, and one in Nevada. See the descriptions in this book of Wyland Galleries in Sarasota and St. Petersburg. His works include numerous large pieces with prices at the high end, some at or over $9,000. Visitors to the Key West gallery have remarked on the close personal attention of the salespeople in the gallery and their willingness to arrange private rooms for consultation about potential purchases. Wyland, a prolific seascape painter, often includes fanciful details in his portrayals of whales and other sea creatures in strikingly clear ocean water. Wyland has established a foundation dedicated to preserving the ocean environment.

Plan your visit: 623 Duval Street, Key West, (305) 292-4998.

GALLERIES: DUVAL STREET—700 BLOCK

Art on Duval Key West

"Art on Duval Key West, a Procaccini Gallery" was created by Key West photo artist Michael Procaccini. The shop was opened in 2017, following an early smaller venture on Green Street, near the docks for cruise ships. The gallery features works of art created by both local and international artists and photographers. The art offered for sale in the gallery includes both original oil and acrylic paintings, and also features signed and numbered limited-edition giclée prints as well as photographs. Prices are clearly posted, and the works are offered from the moderate to high-moderate price range. Michael Procaccini, the artist-owner, features his own works and those of others with ties to Key West.

Plan your visit: 714 Duval Street, Key West, (305) 741-7001.

GALLERIES: DUVAL STREET—1000 BLOCK

Wild Side Gallery

Wild Side is actually larger than it looks from the street, because it is long, narrow, and deep. Items for sale include pottery, pictures, paintings, and other forms of art with animals as the subject; prices range from medium to high medium for small items.

Plan your visit: 1000 Duval Street, Key West, (305) 296-7800.

Gingerbread Square Gallery

This gallery shows art by about twenty-four artists, mostly painters in styles reminiscent of Van Gogh (i.e., postim-pressionist/plein air), with one or two sculptors and one or two ceramic artists. The gallery is situated in a neighborhood of Victorian homes, boutiques, and restaurants, and itself is in a Victorian structure with a private courtyard. The gallery was originally founded in 1974 by a former mayor of Key West, Richard

Heyman. The gallery continues to focus on works reflecting aspects of local color, including the semitropical environment and the town's multicultural heritage.

Plan your visit: 1207 Duval Street, Key West, (305) 296-8900.

Alan S. Maltz Gallery

This one-person gallery shows the work of Alan Maltz, "official wildlife and fine art photographer for the state of Florida."

Plan your visit: 1210 Duval Street, Key West, (305) 294-0005.

GALLERIES: OFF THE BEATEN PATH

Gallery on Greene

Among other local art, this gallery maintains a collection of Mario Sanchez prints, as well as other works by local Key West artists and Cuban artists.

Plan your visit: 606 Greene Street, Key West, Phone (305) 294-1669.

Harrison Gallery

Founded by Helen and Ben Harrison in 1986, the gallery offers works by themselves and other local artists.

Plan your visit: 825 White Street, Key West, (305) 294-0609.

7 Artists and Friends

This shop currently lists fourteen artists, apparently the original seven plus others in a cooperative or collaborative-style gallery.

Plan your visit: 713 Simonton Street, Key West, (305) 294-8444.

Galleries of Key West

This facility also houses "Books and Books"; the large-scale enterprise

provides "collaborative space," that is, studios for visiting artists as well as lectures, workshops, residencies, and partnership projects for local and aspiring artists. In recent years, the organization has hosted annual studio tours in the month of May to observe the resident artists at work.

Plan your visit: 523 Eaton Street, Key West, Phone (305) 296-0458.

Key West Art Center

This community art center, which had its beginnings in 1960, traces its ancestry back to the New Deal art center established under the local administration of Julius Stone as described above. Today the center focuses on offering space to local artists, usually with inexpensive prints and paintings reflecting the homes, natural environment, and culture of Key West.

Plan your visit: 301 Front Street, Key West, (305) 294-1241.

Dog Tired Studio and Gallery

This gallery is owned and operated by artist Sean P. Callahan, and the shop features a range of watercolors, oils, acrylics, mixed media, blown glass, and photography. Callahan usually hosts the gallery, and he is available to paint portraits of guests' dogs. The gallery's prices are in the low to moderate range.

Plan your visit: 1101 Whitehead Street, Key West, (802) 989-5910.

Gildea Contemporary Art Gallery

This gallery was established in 2013 and currently hosts the work of about nineteen artists and sculptors.

Plan your visit: 522 Southard Street, Key West, (305) 797-6485.

Rockhouse Gallery

This unusual gallery sells one-of-a-kind contemporary furniture and, currently, works by four artists: Aaron Chang, Tony Ludovico, Joan Becker, and Carol Mc-Ardle. The visual art is either seascape/ tropical wildlife or colorful/decorator pieces. The gallery also rents out space for receptions and private parties.

Plan your visit: 330 Julia Street, Key West, (305) 600-7823.

Afterword:
Other hidden gems, neighborhoods, and museums

In addition to all the cities and towns that have an active art presence that we present in detail in this book, there are a dozen or more communities and neighborhoods in Florida that share in the state's reputation as a refuge for artists, sculptors, and other creative people. For example, on the long drive to Key West along Highway 1, which leapfrogs from island to island following the old pathway of Henry Flagler's "over the sea" rail link, visitors pass through three small communities (Key Largo, Marathon, and Islamorada) noted as boating and fishing getaways, each the home of several artists, with occasional galleries along the way.

Other towns, both large and small, some of them magnets for tourists, notable beach resorts, or known as destinations for retirees or snowbirds, each have practicing artists, galleries, art classes and studios, art centers, and other outlets for art. Several host annual art shows that draw thousands of visitors.

On the Gulf coast, these towns all lay claim to status as art destinations, each with its own unique ambience: Cedar Key, Dunedin, Venice, and Matlacha.

In central Florida, the town of Micanopy hosts several art outlets, and its charm and cracker heritage attract academics from nearby Gainesville as well as tourists from all over the world.

Several of the "beach resort" large towns on the Atlantic coast—Daytona Beach, Palm Beach, and Fort Lauderdale—also have attracted both artists and art patrons.

These are among the many communities and neighborhoods throughout the state that we were not able to cover in detail, all of which have art destination reputations. We leave these and other hidden gems for the reader to discover and explore.

In addition, we provide below addresses and phone numbers of smaller or specialized art museums in the state, listed by town.

Avon Park: Peter Powell Roberts Museum of Art, 310 West Main Avenue, (863) 453-4531

Boca Raton: Boca Raton Museum of Art, 501 Plaza Real, (561) 392-2500

Coral Gables: Lowe Art Museum, 1301 Stanford Drive, (305) 284-3535

Coral Springs: Coral Springs Museum of Art, 2855a Coral Springs Drive, (954) 340-5000

Daytona Beach: Cici and Hyatt Brown Museum of Art, and Daytona Museum of Arts and Science, (colocated at) 352 South Nova Road, (386) 255-0285

Deland: Museum of Art, 600 North Woodland Boulevard, (386) 734-4371; Downtown: 100 North Woodland Boulevard, (386) 279-7534

Delray Beach: Morikami Museum and Japanese Garden, 4000 Morikami Park Road, (561) 496-0233

Fort Lauderdale: Nova Southeastern University Art Museum, 1 East Las Olas Boulevard, (954) 525-5500

Hollywood: Art and Culture Center of Hollywood, 1650 Harrison Street, (954) 721-3274

Lake Eustis/Tavares: Lake County Museum of Art, 213 West Ruby Street, (352) 483-2900

Ormand Beach: Ormand Memorial Art Museum, 78 East Granada Boulevard, (386) 676-3374

Palm Beach: Society of the Four Arts, 102 Four Arts Plaza, (561) 655-7226

Sebring: Highlands Museum of Art, 351 West Centre Avenue, (863) 385-5312

St. Petersburg: Imagine Museum, 1901 Central Avenue, (727) 300-1700

Tarpon Springs: Leeper-Rattner Museum of Art, 600 East Klosterman Road, (727) 712-5762

Vero Beach: Vero Beach Museum of Art, 3001 Riverside Drive, (772) 231-0707

West Palm Beach: Ann Norton Sculpture Gardens, 253 Barcelona Road, (561) 832-5328

West Palm Beach: Norton Museum of Art, 1450 South Dixie Highway, (561) 832-5196

Further Reading

Descriptive materials in this guide of art museums, centers, galleries, and individual works of art are derived from visits to the sites; from discussion with museum, art center, and gallery personnel; from literature such as guides, flyers, and brochures issued by the museums, galleries and art centers; and from descriptions of the sites and institutions published online. Most art museums also provide, for each work of art shown, accompanying descriptive material about the artist and the piece of work, its provenance, and, sometimes, the art genre to which it belongs, and we took note of many such descriptive panels.

In addition, several published sources on art colonies more generally, works on Florida history, and art in Florida have proven useful.

Buck, Pat Ringling, with Marcia Corbino and Kevin Dean. *A History of Visual Art in Sarasota.* Gainesville: University Press of Florida, 2003.

Frank, Nance. *Mario Sanchez, Better Than Ever.* Sarasota, FL: Pineapple, 2010.

Jeffrey, Anne E. F., and Aletta D. Dreller. *Art Lover's Guide to Florida.* Sarasota, FL: Pineapple, 1998.

Knowlton, Christopher. *Bubble in the Sun: The Florida Boom of the 1920s and How It Brought on the Great Depression.* New York: Simon and Schuster, 2020.

Libby, Gary Russell. *Reflections: Paintings of Florida, 1865–1965.* Daytona Beach, FL: Museum of Arts and Sciences, 2009.

Mann, Maybelle. *Art in Florida, 1564–1945.* Sarasota, FL: Pineapple, 1999.

McIver, Stuart. *Hemingway's Key West.* 2nd ed. Sarasota, FL: Pineapple, 2012.

Shipp, Steve. *American Art Colonies, 1850–1930: A Historical Guide to America's Original Art Colonies and Their Artists.* Westport, CT: Greenwood, 1996.

Smith, Jules André. *In France with the American Expeditionary Forces.* New York: Arthur H. Halo, 1919 (available online).

Torchia, Robert W. *Lost Colony: The Artists of St. Augustine, 1930–1950.* St. Augustine, FL: Lightner Museum, 2001 (available online).

ART CENTER, COMMUNITY, AND MUSEUM PERIODIC PUBLICATIONS

A number of institutions and communities issue periodic publications; those we consulted are listed below.

ArtCenter Manatee 2019–20 Fall–Winter Classes and Workshops. ArtCenter Manatee, Bradenton, Florida.

Art Center Sarasota Exhibition Gallery Guide, 2019–2020: Open Season National Juried Exhibition. Sarasota, Florida.

Art.i.facts. Volume 22, no. 1, December 2019–January 2020. Polk Arts Alliance, Bartow, Florida.

artifacts. September–December 2019, College of Central Florida, Appleton Museum of Art, Ocala, Florida.

Artis-Naples: 100 Iconic Works from the Permanent Collection, December 1, 2019–July 25, 2020. Artis-Naples, Naples, Florida.

Calendar of Events. Winter 2020. Atlantic Center for the Arts, New Smyrna Beach, Florida.

Cornell Fine Arts Museum, Fall 2019 Exhibitions and Programming. Rollins College, Winter Park, Florida.

Exhibitions and Programs at the Morse Museum, 2019–2020 Guide. Charles Hosmer Morse Foundation, Winter Park, Florida.

Forma MoCA Jacksonville. Fall–Winter 2019–2020. Semiannual. Museum of Contemporary Art, Jacksonville, Florida.

Mount Dora Living. August 2019. Best Version Media, Brookfield, Wisconsin.

The Murals of Lake Placid Florida. Volume 20, 2019. Lake Placid Mural Society, Lake Placid, Florida.

Orlando Arts Magazine. January/February 2020. United Arts of Central Florida, Maitland, Florida.

Studio Art Programs Fall 2019–Spring 2020. College of Central Florida, Appleton Museum of Art, Ocala, Florida.

Village of the Arts Map and Business Directory, 2019. Artists Guild of Manatee, Bradenton, Florida.

About the Authors

Rodney and Loretta Carlisle are the coauthors of a series of historical guidebooks to the following cities, all with Pineapple Press: Charleston, South Carolina; Savannah, Georgia; and St. Augustine, Key West, Tampa, and Tallahassee, Florida. In addition, they coauthored *Forts of Florida*. Rodney Carlisle is professor emeritus from Rutgers University with publications on a wide variety of subjects, including maritime history and maritime art; Loretta Carlisle is a widely published photographer.